Martin Arnold * DEANIMATED

Herausgeber:

GERALD MATT | THOMAS MIESSGANG | **KUNSTHALLE** wien

Vorwort

Gerald Matt

Preface

Gerald Matt

Warum macht eine Kunsthalle eine Ausstellung mit einem Regisseur? Eine Präsentation, bei der keine Bilder, keine Skulpturen, keine Fotos zu sehen sind, sondern nur drei installative Einheiten, in denen Filme gezeigt werden?

Vor fünfzehn, zwanzig Jahren wäre diese Frage noch einer profunden Erörterung wert gewesen, doch mittlerweile sind wir daran gewöhnt, dass die Bilder auch im Ausstellungshaus zu laufen begonnen haben: Andy Warhol entdeckte schon in den sechziger Jahren den Film als expressives Strategem, jüngere Künstler wie Shirin Neshat, Steve McQueen oder Zarina Bhimji konzentrieren sich in noch stärkerem Maße auf dieses Medium. Was die Ausstellung *Deanimated* von den schon etablierten Präsentationen bewegter Bilder im Biotop der Bildenden Kunst unterscheidet, ist die Tatsache, dass Martin Arnold einem anderen Milieu zugerechnet wird: dem des experimentellen Films. Er ist somit einer der ersten Regisseure, die aus der Guckkastensituation des traditionellen Kinos heraustreten und ihre Arbeit rezeptionsästhetisch neu definieren: Zwingen auch die avanciertesten Filmkunstwerke dem Publikum eine konventionelle Betrachtersituation auf, so ermöglicht Arnold den Besuchern die Emanzipation vom Kinosessel (den es in der Ausstellung gleichwohl auch gibt). Die für diese Präsentation neu hergestellten Arbeiten *Deanimated - The Invisible Ghost, Forsaken* und *Dissociated* arbeiten mit desorientierenden Taktiken wie Doppelprojektionen und spatialer Klangauffächerung und schaffen die Rahmenbedingungen für eine Ästhetik der verstohlenen Blicke und der flüchtigen Wahrnehmung. Das fokussierte Auge kann nicht mehr ALLES sehen (auch wenn das im Lichtspieltheater schon eine Illusion war), es muss sich de-zentralisieren, neu kalibrieren, um im Surplus der kinematographischen Ereignisse individuelle Blickachsen zu finden und in der Fülle simultaner visueller Abläufe seine subjektive Kombinatorik zu betreiben.

Martin Arnold hat den Schritt in eine Situation, die das Verhältnis von Zuschauer und Objekt in ein neues Verhandlungsverhältnis bringt, bewusst gesetzt: Nachdem er auf der Produktionsseite eine Fülle von visuellen und akustischen Versuchsanordnungen durchdekliniert hat, geht es ihm jetzt darum, auch das rezeptive Tableau einer Investigation zu unterziehen. Die in *Deanimated*, einer Art Palimpsest des alten Horror Movies *The Invisible Ghost* mit Bela Lugosi, praktizierte Kunst des Verschwindens, ein altes Motiv des Detektivfilms, das hier mit digitalen Mitteln aktualisiert wird, überlagert sich mit der Absenz des nicht Wahrgenommenen. Der Topos des Evasiven in der doppelten Ummantelung hat auch Arnolds produktives Prinzip affiziert: Waren die drei Filme, mit denen er seinen Ruhm als meistausgezeichneter österreichischer Avantgarderegisseur der Gegenwart begründet hat (*pièce touchée, passage à l'acte, Alone*)

Why would an art centre put on an exhibition involving a film director? A presentation featuring no pictures, no sculptures, no photographs, only three units of installations, where films are being shown?

Fifteen, twenty years ago, this question might still have warranted a profound discussion, but in the meantime we have become accustomed to the fact that even in an exhibition space the pictures have learned to walk. Andy Warhol discovered film as an expressive stratagem as far back as the early sixties, while younger artists like Shirin Neshat, Steve McQueen or Zarina Bhimji have been concentrating even more strongly on this medium in recent times. What distinguishes the *Deanimated* exhibition from established presentations of moving images within the biotope of the visual arts is the fact that Martin Arnold is usually associated with another taxonomic pond, that of the experimental film. He is thus one of the first directors to step outside the looking-glass situation of traditional cinema and to define afresh the aesthetics of their work's perception. While even the most advanced works of cinematic art impose a conventional viewing situation upon their audiences, Arnold offers his visitors an emancipation from the theatre seat (which, nonetheless, can be found at the exhibition, as well). The works newly created for this presentation, *Deanimated - The Invisible Ghost, Forsaken* and *Dissociated*, operate with disorientating tactics such as dual projections and a spatial fanning-out of the soundtrack, which contribute to a framework of conditions for an aesthetic of the furtive glance and the tangential perception. The focusing eye can no longer see EVERYTHING (even if this was already an illusion in the movie theatre), it has to de-centralise itself, recalibrate itself, in order to find individual viewing axes within the surplus of cinematographic events and to engage in its own subjective combinatorics within the profusion of simultaneously occurring visual events.

It was a conscious decision on the part of Martin Arnold to take the step of entering into a situation, which moved the relationship between the spectator and the object into a newly-negotiated realm, and after declensing a plethora of visual and acoustic test series on the production side, his aim now is to subject the receptive tableau to an investigation, as well. The art of making objects disappear, as practised in *Deanimated*, a kind of palimpsest on the old horror movie, *The Invisible Ghost*, featuring Bela Lugosi, is an old motif of detective films, which has here been given a new lease of live by digital means, and which overlaps with the absence of the unperceived. The topic of the evasive within a double coating has also affected Arnold's productive principle. While the three films upon which his fame is based as the most highly decorated Austrian avant-garde film director of the present time (*pièce touchée, passage à l'acte, Alone*), breathless stop-and-go vehicles

atemlose Stop and Go-Vehikel auf der Folie konventioneller amerikanischer Spielfilme, die im Flickern der Ereignisse Spuren des Unbewussten und des Erotischen freisetzten, so hat *Deanimated* einen ruhigeren Atem. Die Personen werden nicht mehr im Moment ihrer hysterischen Dekomposition erfasst, sondern im Augenblick des Verstummens, der sprachlosen Gegenüberstellung. Dort, wo im Thriller die nahtlose Verknüpfung der Worte kommunikatives Gelingen suggeriert, bedeutet reale Gegenwart in Arnolds Film den unbenennbaren Horror der stummen Konfrontation. *Deanimated* nähert sich im Sprachzerfall jenem Nullpunkt der Existenz, wo die Figuren sich selbst beim Verlöschen zusehen.

Ich freue mich, dass die Kunsthalle Wien den archetypischen ‚symptomatischen' Regisseur der Gegenwart an einer Peripetie seines Schaffens zeigen kann; einem Wendepunkt, wo sich das Verdrängte der Hollywood-Maschine in neuen Formen und gestischen Idiomen manifestiert. „Farben, Kontraste und Rhythmen berühren den Betrachter nicht im Bereich der Sprache und der Logik", hat Martin Arnold einmal gesagt. „Sie kommunizieren auf tieferen Ebenen. Ich würde den Diskurs, an dem sie teilnehmen, im Bereich des Unbewussten situieren."

all, based on the foil of conventional American entertainment films, which, in the flickering of events, liberate traces of the unconscious and the erotic, *Deanimated* has a calmer air. Individuals are no longer caught at the moment of their hysterical decomposition, but at the instant of falling into silence, of a speechless juxtaposition. At the point where, in a thriller, the seamless conjunction of the words suggests a communicative success, the real presence in Arnold's film signifies the unnamed horror of dumbfounded confrontation. *Deanimated* approaches, in its disintegration of language, that zero point of existence where the characters are busy watching their own effacement.

I am gladdened by the fact that Kunsthalle Wien is able to show this archetypally 'symptomatic' director of our time at a peripatetic crossroads of his creative activity, a turning point, where the repressive aspects of the Hollywood machine manifest themselves in new forms and gestural idioms. "Colours, contrasts and rhythms do not touch the spectator in the sphere of language or logic," Martin Arnold has once said. "They communicate at deeper levels. I would situate the discourse, in which they participate, within the realm of the unconscious."

DANK

Thomas Miessgang, Kurator der Kunsthalle Wien, hat in enger Kooperation mit Martin Arnold die Grundidee für die Ausstellung entwickelt und so lange am Konzept herumgebastelt, bis es schließlich in das Prokrustesbett des Budgets passte. Die Filmproduktion Amour Fou, im besonderen Alexander Dumreicher-Ivanceanu und Gabriele Kranzelbinder, ermöglichte die Herstellung der drei neuen Arbeiten Arnolds und lieferte mit perfektem Last-Minute-Timing die unverzichtbare Software für die Ausstellung *Deanimated*. Der Architekt Georg Driendl erdachte ein schlüssiges Konzept, das die Bedürfnisse von Filmprojektion und Raumgliederung perfekt aufeinander abstimmte. Einen wichtigen Beitrag zur Ausstellung lieferten auch Walter Pamminger, der ein Katalogkonzept entwickelte, das die Essenz der Filme ins Medium Buch transferiert, ohne schlichte Bebilderung zu sein, und Anna Bertermann, die diese graphische Idee kongenial umsetzte. Weiters möchte ich auch dem Team der Kunsthalle Wien danken, im besonderen Sigrid Mittersteiner (kuratorische Assistenz), Michael Ziegert (Produktionsleitung) sowie Paul Lehner und Ramon Villalobos (Technik), die im Finish beachtliche Kräfte freisetzten, um noch vor der Deadline über die Ziellinie zu kommen.

THANKS

Thomas Miessgang, curator of Kunsthalle Wien, in close cooperation with Martin Arnold, developed the fundamental idea of the exhibition and jiggled the concept long enough for it to finally fit into the procrustean budgetary framework. Alexander Dumreicher-Ivanceanu and Gabriele Kranzelbinder, of the Amour Fou film company took care of the production of Arnold's three latest works and delivered, with perfect last-minute timing, the indispensable soft-ware for the exhibition *Deanimated*. The architect Georg Driendl put together a coherent concept, which perfectly matched the mutual requirements of film projection and spatial arrangements. An important contribution to the exhibition was also made by Walter Pamminger, who developed a concept for the catalogue that successfully transfers the essence of the films into the medium of the book without reducing it to a mere case of illustration, and by Anna Bertermann, who equally ingeniously turned this graphic idea into a reality. Further to this, my thanks are owed to the team of the Kunsthalle Wien, in particular, Sigrid Mittersteiner (curatorial assistance), Michael Ziegert (production management), as well as Paul Lehner and Ramon Villalobos (technical wizardry) who all managed to release unbounded energies in the completion stages in order to come in at the finish before the deadline.

Zum Visualisierungskonzept von *Deanimated*

Walter Pamminger

Regarding the Visualisation Concept of *Deanimated*

Walter Pamminger

Mein gestalterischer Grundansatz war die Synchronisation von Film und Buch durch ein fortlaufendes Diagramm. Ein Punkt bzw. Strich dieser diagrammatischen Spur repräsentiert den *Speicherplatz* von einer Sekunde Film. Der daraus jeweils ausgewählte Filmkader steht stellvertretend für eine ganze Einstellung, wobei dessen Größe sich nach der Szenenlänge bemisst.

Aus diesem Drängen der Zeit im filmischem Bild resultiert eine doppelte Ikonizität: neben filmischen Inhalten werden auch Aspekte der Dauer visualisiert. Dies bedeutet die Preisgabe eines zentralen Bereiches gestalterischer Tätigkeit: der kontrollierten Skalierung und Platzierung der Bild-Dokumente im Rahmen des Buches. Der Film in seinen Zeitformaten layoutet sich gleichsam automatisch entlang der diagrammatischen Spur, das Buch wiederum schneidet das filmische Dokument - bisweilen auch dort, wo der Film nie geschnitten werden darf: innerhalb eines Kaders. Bereits als Gestalter wurde ich so zum gespannten Beobachter eines konzeptuell induzierten Prozesses der raumzeitlichen Reflexion eines Filmes im Medium des Buches.

My design principle was to synchronise the film and the book through a continuous diagram. One dot or dash on this diagrammatic track represents the *storage location* of one second of film. The individual frame selected in each case is representative of an entire shot, its size being dependent upon the length of the scene.

This pressure of time upon the cinematic image results in a dual iconicity, visualising both the film's content and also aspects of its duration. This means that a central area of design work, the controlled scaling and placing of pictorial documents within the frame of the book, has to be relinquished. Film, in its time formats, lays itself out automatically, of sorts, along that diagrammatic trail, whereas the book cuts up the cinematic document, sometimes even at a point where a film must never be cut, in the middle of a frame. As a designer I became an excited observer early on of a conceptually-induced process of temporal-spatial reflection upon a film within the medium of the book.

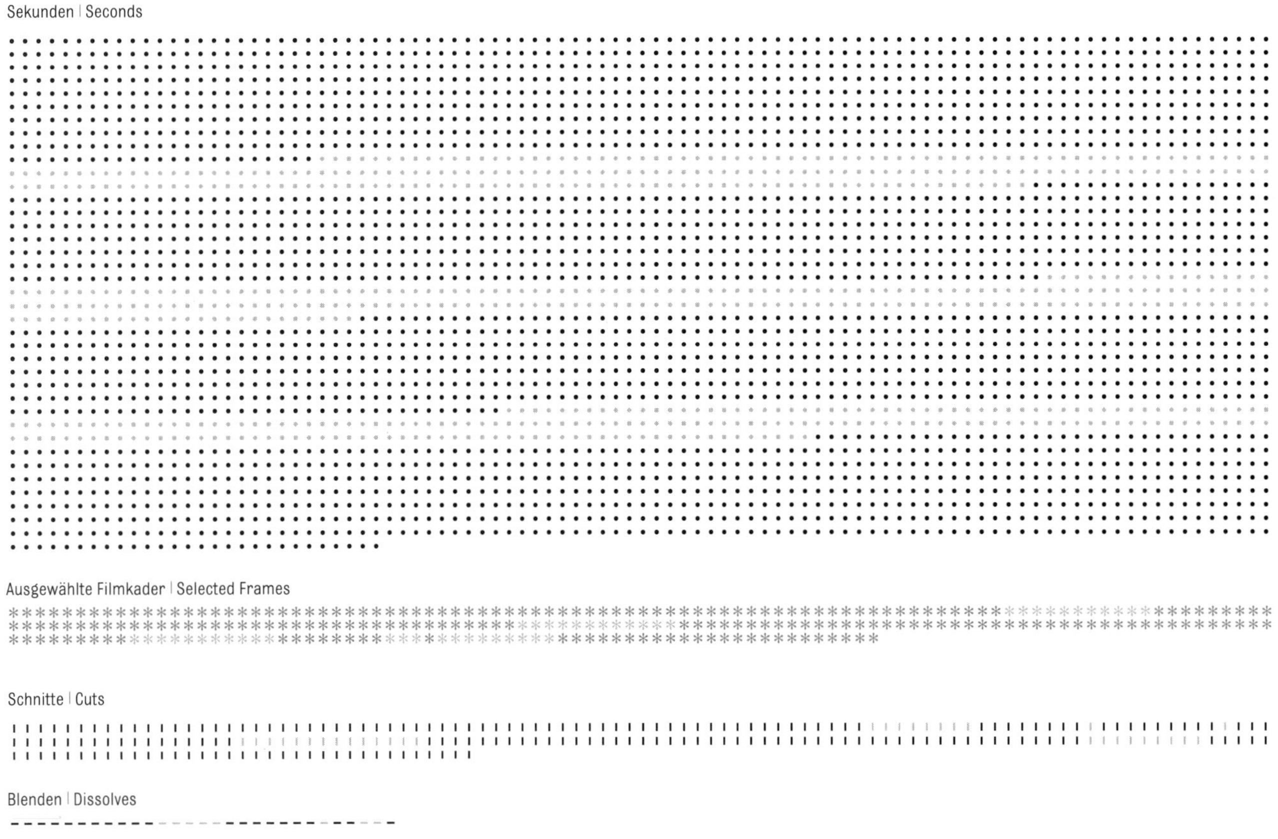

Sekunden | Seconds

Ausgewählte Filmkader | Selected Frames

Schnitte | Cuts

Blenden | Dissolves

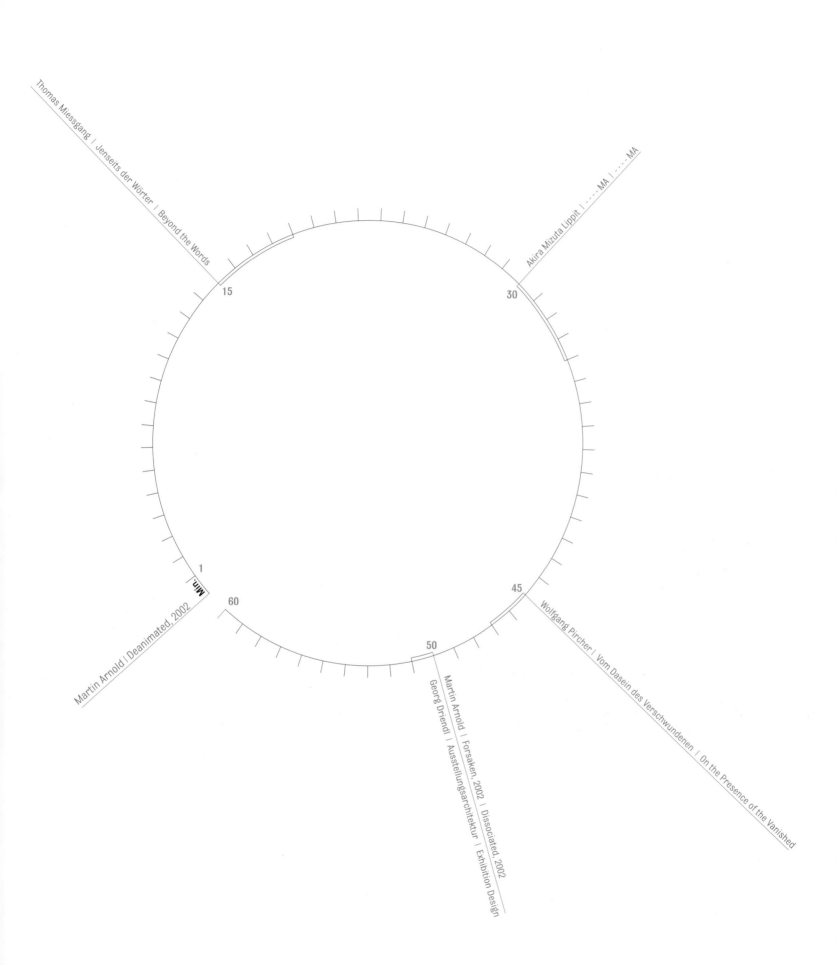

Thomas Miessgang | Jenseits der Wörter | Beyond the Words

Akira Mizuta Lippit | – – – MA | – – – – MA

Martin Arnold | Deanimated, 2002

Min.

1

15

60

30

45

50

Wolfgang Pircher | Vom Dasein des Verschwundenen | On the Presence of the Vanished

Martin Arnold | Forsaken, 2002 | Dissociated, 2002
Georg Driendl | Ausstellungsarchitektur | Exhibition Design

DEANIMATED (The Invisible Ghost), 2002

Schwarzweiß-Film auf DVD, 5-Kanal Ton
Rauminstallation, Projektionsfläche 6 x 4,50 m
Loop-Dauer: 60 min |

Black-and-white film on DVD, 5-channel sound
Spatial installation, projection screen 6 x 4.50 m
Loop duration: 60 min

D W. ROTE

M. SAETA

SLOTT

LE PICARD

GOULD

GOLDEN

ED PREBLE

RTER, A.S.C.A.P.

NN

Approved

ATION

CERTIFICATE
Nº 7243

The Cast

Mr. Kessler	BELA LUGOSI
Virginia	POLLY ANN YOUNG
Ralph	JOHN McGUIRE
Paul	
Evans	CLARENCE MUSE
Cecile	TERRY WALKER
Mrs. Kessler	BETTY COMPSON
Jules	ERNIE ADAMS
Williams	GEORGE PEMBROKE
Mrs. Mason	OLLOLA NESMITH
Ryan	FRED KELSEY
Tim	JACK MULHALL

Produced by
SAM KATZMAN
BANNER PICTURES CORP.

Directed
JOSEPH H. L

* * *

Good evening, Evans.

Good evening, my dear.

You're more beautiful than ever this evening.

Evans, how is dad taking it?

I told you not to come here this evening.

Why, didn't you want to see me?

You're certainly acting strange, darling.

Let's go in the library.

Ralph!

After dinner, we're taking a long walk.

It struck me cold.

I'm sorry if I accidentally stumbled on something you didn't want me to know.

He always appeared perfectly rational to me.

There's something I must tell you.

I don't understand.

Well, it happened several years ago.

Father worshipped me.

It almost broke my father's heart.

Ohhh.

I'm gonna take a drive. Such a beautiful night, come along?

Sure, you don't mind going?

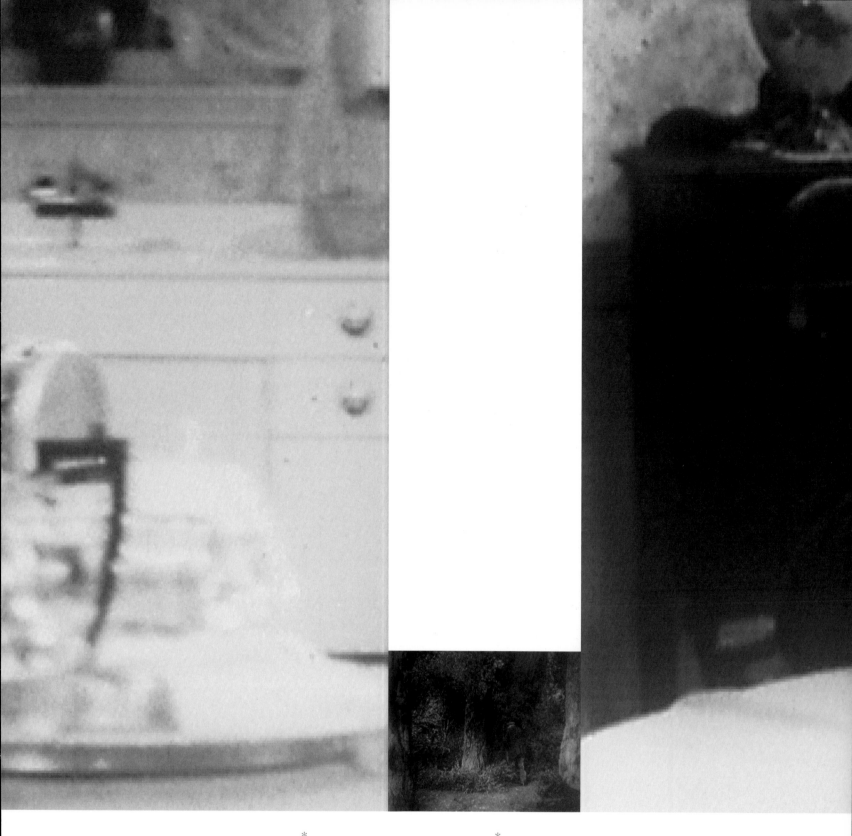

*   *

You're late again.

*

Sure you won't come in?

Good night.

Oh, Virginia!

Would you please put my car in the garage,

when you have a moment?

Guess what?

I'm so happy with you my dear.

Good night, my dad.

Good night, sweetie.

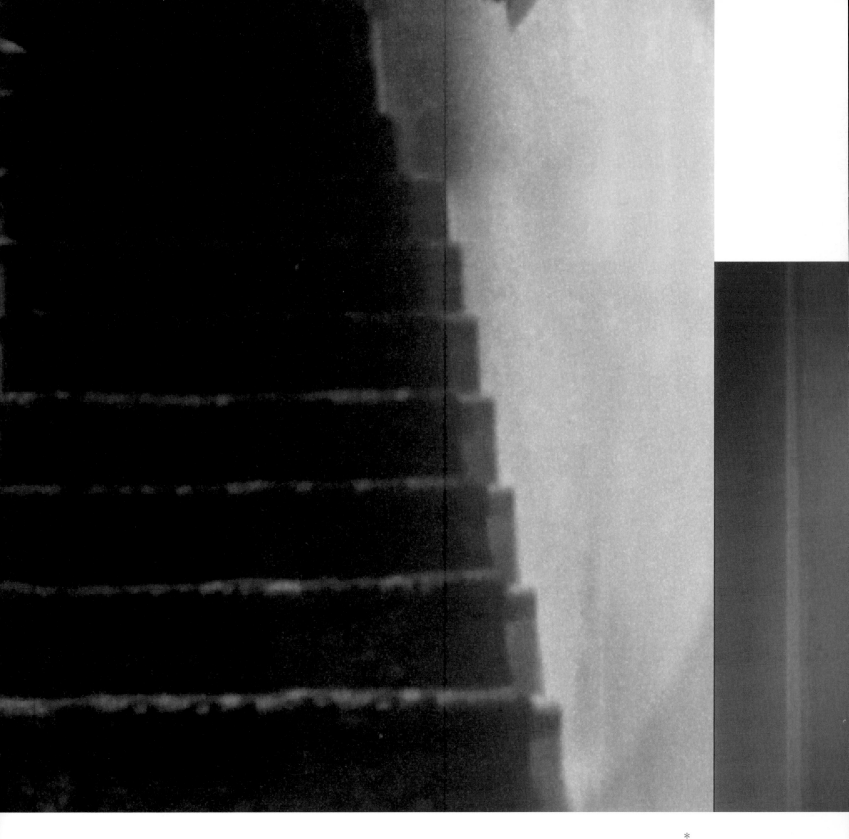

*

Jenseits der Wörter

Die multiplen Erzählungen des Filmemachers Martin Arnold

Thomas Miessgang

Generell ist das Verhältnis des Blicks zu dem, was man sehen möchte, ein Verhältnis des Trugs. Das Subjekt stellt sich als etwas anderes dar, als es ist, und was man ihm zu sehen gibt, ist nicht, was es zu sehen wünscht. (Jacques Lacan)

Martin Arnold gehört nicht zu den Künstlern, die den öffentlichen Aufmerksamkeitsraum mit Produktionen überfluten. Seine Filmographie umfasst zwei Frühwerke, die er nicht mehr gerne zeigt, da er sie für unfertige Vorstufen seiner gereiften Ästhetik hält (O.T.-1 und O.T.-2), mehrere Trailer und drei mittellange Arbeiten, die seinen Ruhm als Innovator des experimentellen Films begründet haben: *pièce touchée, passage à l'acte und Alone. Life Wastes Andy Hardy.*

Dazu kommen jetzt die drei Installationen, aus denen die Ausstellung *Deanimated* der Kunsthalle Wien komponiert ist, und die die Rezeptionssituation neu definieren: Der Zuschauer ist nicht mehr an den Kinosessel gefesselt, sondern er wird ‚mobilisiert': In einem System aus Doppelprojektionen und dislozierten Klangereignissen kann er sich nach Gutdünken bewegen, seine eigenen Zeitmaße festlegen und individuelle Navigationen entwerfen. Martin Arnold begibt sich damit, von der Seite des Filmemachers kommend, in ein Arrangement das in der Bildenden Kunst - man denke etwa an Andy Warhols ‚Galerienfilme' wie *Empire* - schon seit Jahrzehnten geläufig ist und in den neunziger Jahren noch ausgebaut wurde. Der Einzug des Films ins Museum habe das Zwielicht mit sich gebracht, sagt der Kulturtheoretiker Boris Groys, und verlängere die Ausstellungen potentiell ins Unendliche: „Der Zuseher wird zum Flaneur, zu einem fast zufälligen Zeugen eines Vorganges, den er nur noch zum Teil überblicken kann. Er wirft einen schnellen Blick auf das Objekt und geht dann wieder weg. Das ist die Kunst der verstohlenen Blicke und der kurzen Begegnungen." Groys spricht in diesem Zusammenhang auch von einer „partiellen Invisibilität" des Films, was wiederum die künstlerische Intention der Ausstellung *Deanimated*, die um die Metaphern des Verschwindens und Verstummens gewebt ist, auf die Achse des Besucherblickes hin verlängert.

Beyond the Words

The multiple narratives of the filmmaker Martin Arnold

Thomas Miessgang

Generally the relation of the glance to that which it wishes to see is a relation of deception. The subject presents itself as something other than what it is, and what it is given to see is not what it wishes to see. (Jacques Lacan)

Martin Arnold is not one of those artists who flood the public attention space with their productions. His filmography comprises two early works (Untitled 1 and Untitled 2), which he no longer likes to show, as he considers them to be incomplete advance stages of his mature aesthetic; several trailers and three works of medium-length, upon which his fame as a prime innovator of experimental film are founded: *pièce touchée, passage à l'acte* and *Alone. Life Wastes Andy Hardy.*

In addition, there now exist three installations, which comprise the exhibition *Deanimated* at the Kunsthalle Wien, and which newly define the situation of his reception by the public. The viewer is no longer chained to the cinema seat, but is, rather, 'mobilised', being enabled to move at will within a system of dual projections and dislocated sound events, which allow for the discovery of one's own time measures and the devising of individual navigational schemes. Martin Arnold has thus moved, coming from the other side, from filmmaking, into an arrangement, which has been commonplace in the visual arts for decades - certainly since Andy Warhol's 'films to be shown in galleries', such as *Empire*, an arrangement that has been extended considerably during the '90s. The introduction of films into the museum has ushered in a twilight zone, according to cultural theoretician Boris Groys, who sees a potential extension of exhibitions into infinity: "The viewer becomes an idle loiterer, an almost accidental witness to a process he can only partially grasp. He casts a quick glance at the object, and then moves on again. This is the art of the furtive glance and fleeting encounters." Groys also talks about a 'partial invisibility' of film, which in turn reflects the artistic intention of the exhibition *Deanimated* which is woven around metaphors for the disappearance and dissolution of speech, extended along the axis of the visitor's gaze.

AUSLÖSCHUNG

Die Modifikation im Verhältnis des Publikums zum Werk von der immobilen Guckkastensituation zum schrittweisen Erkunden unterschiedlicher Räume und Zeitfalten berührt auch den produktiven Kern von Martin Arnolds Gestaltungsparadigma: *Deanimated - The Invisible Ghost,* das zentrale Werk der Ausstellung, ist mit 60 Minuten rund viermal so lang wie seine älteren Filme und von erheblich geringerer Ereignisdichte. Während die mittlerweile kanonische Trilogie die Idee von der *information overload* durch visuelle und akustische Überforderung durchspielt, so gönnt sich *Deanimated* den Luxus der gestischen und narrativen Auszehrung: Personen der Handlung wurden herausgelöscht, die dadurch entstandenen Löcher im Bild mit den Mitteln des *digital compositing* wieder aufgefüllt. Dialoge fallen zu dürren Satzfragmenten oder Appellationen ohne Antwort zusammen, Musik braust auf, um Nicht-Ereignisse enthusiastisch zu blähen. Der *Invisible Ghost* des Originalfilms von Joseph H. Lewis wird in der Überschreibung durch Martin Arnold zum Schattenriss des Verschwindens, zu einer unheimlichen Präsenz des Absenten, dessen irreale Gegenwart sich in den unsicheren Suchbewegungen der Kamera in leeren Räumen manifestiert.

Deanimated ist Arnolds bewusste Entscheidung, eine Linie weiterzuschreiben, die er mit *Alone. Life Wastes Andy Hardy* begonnen hat: Die Schrauben an der Intensitätsmaschinerie, die die Kompressionsästhetik der ersten beiden Filme definierte, wurden gelockert: die Mikro-Erzählungen in den Eingeweiden der vom Künstler bearbeiteten Originalausrisse können sich freizügiger und weiträumiger entfalten. Die *back and forth-*Ästhetik, der visuelle Hip Hop des Bilder-Scratching - Arnolds Trademark - wurde schon bei *Alone* sparsamer eingesetzt, bei *Deanimated* ist sie völlig verschwunden.

Solch radikale Richtungswechsel haben auch damit zu tun, dass der Künstler seine Arbeiten als Versuchsanordnungen auffasst: In minuziöser Detailarbeit wird ein a priori gesetztes Prinzip durchdekliniert und in all seinen Facetten ausgelotet. Die Investition an Arbeitszeit ist enorm, das Resultat eine so hochkonzentrierte Verdichtung, dass jede Wiederholung wie ein flaues Da Capo wirken würde. Ging es bei *pièce touchée* um die Kaderfür-Kader Analyse einer 18-Sekunden-Einstellung bei asynchroner Tonspur, so wurde bei *passage à l'acte* das Verhältnis von Bild und Klang im Setting einer virtuellen Familienszene getestet. *Alone* wiederum befasste sich mit Exaltationen des Gefühls und deren filmischer Modulierbarkeit und *Deanimated* mit der Entvölkerung von Räumen, der Entseelung von Szenarien und deren gleichzeitiger Aufladung mit negativer Energie, mit einer Art Anti-Materie des Seins.

EFFACEMENT

The modification in the relationship between the audience and the work from the immobile situation of the magic lantern in the darkened room to the step-by-step exploration of diverse spaces and time-warps also affects the productive centre of Martin Arnold's creative paradigm. *Deanimated - The Invisible Ghost*, the central work of the exhibition, at 60 minutes is about four times as long as his older films and of considerably lower event-density. While what has become a canonic trilogy plays up the idea of information overload through visual and acoustic demands on the viewer's constant attention, *Deanimated* allows itself the luxury of gestural and narrative consumptiveness. The characters of the plot were effaced, and the resultant holes in the picture filled up again by means of digital compositing. Dialogues collapse into sparse phrasal fragments or appellations without reply, music flares up, swelling non-events with enthusiasm. The "*invisible ghost*" of the original film by Joseph. H. Lewis turns, in Martin Arnold's overwrite, into a shadowy silhouette of evanescence, an uncanny presence of the absent, whose irrationally unreal existence manifests itself in the tentative searching movements of the camera within vacant rooms.

Deanimated represents Arnold's conscious decision to continue his writing along the lines he had started with in *Alone. Life Wastes Andy Hardy.* The screws on the machinery of intensity, which defined the compressive aesthetic of his first two films, were loosened, the micro-narratives within the innards of the clippings taken from the original and re-worked by the artist can now unfold more liberally and more extensively. The *back-and-forth* aesthetics, the visual hip-hop of picture scratching - Arnold's trademark - were already being employed more sparingly in *Alone*, and have completely disappeared from *Deanimated.*

Such radical changes in direction are also connected with the fact that the artist perceives his works as experimental arrangements, where a principle, once established, is investigated in minute detail and explored in all its facets. The investment in working hours is enormous, and the result a such highly-concentrated compression of material as to cause any repetition to appear like a limp *da capo.* If *pièce touchée* was the frame-by-frame analysis of an 18-second sequence with an asynchronous soundtrack, *passage à l'acte* was the test of a relationship between picture and sound in a setting involving a virtual family scene. *Alone*, in turn, dealt with the exaltations of emotions and their cinematic capacity for modulation, while *Deanimated* went into the depopulation of spaces and the removal of the soul from scenarios which were simultaneously charged with negative energy, with a kind of antimatter of existence.

FLATTERN

Die *frame-by-frame*-Methode verweist auf ein von Martin Arnold immer wieder betontes Nahverhältnis zu Peter Kubelka und dessen Versuchen, die unerforschte Essenz des Mediums zu fassen, die geheimen Botschaften zwischen den Kadern zu dechiffrieren. Was den jüngeren Filmemacher allerdings unterscheidet, ist der Bezug auf die Erzählmaschine des klassischen Hollywood-Films aus der Epoche der großen Studios. Damit ist das Ausgangsmaterial seiner Bearbeitungen derart referentiell aufgeladen, dass zwangsläufig eine Dialektik von Geschichte und Gegenwart, von Ausgesprochenem und Verdrängtem, von realer Gegenwart und den Gespenstern des Imaginären entsteht. „Das Hollywood-Kino ist ein Kino des Ausgrenzens, Reduzierens und Verleugnens, ein Kino der Verdrängung," hat Arnold in einem panoramatischen Gespräch mit Scott McDonald gesagt. „Deshalb sollten wir nicht nur das berücksichtigen, was gezeigt wird, sondern auch das, was nicht gezeigt wird."

Trotz aller formalen Entwicklungsschritte in Arnolds Kino gibt es Motive, die seit Beginn seiner Expedition ins Unbewusste der filmischen Repräsentation als fluktuierende Chiffren im Zwielicht der bewegten Bilder nisten: die Erotik von Annäherung und Rückzug, die Idee der Mensch-Maschine, die strafende Hand, das nervöse Zittern der Neurose, der Schatten des Todes.

Diese großen Menschheitsthemen werden nicht explizit ausgestellt, sondern gleiten gleichsam unter der Hand in die Mechanik der streng reglementierten Abläufe. Erinnern wir uns an *pièce touchée*: Ein friedliches Wohnzimmer, eine Frau sitzt auf einem Kanapee und vertieft sich in die Lektüre einer Zeitschrift. Plötzlich beginnt die Tür im Hintergrund zu flattern - ein hysterisches Auf und Zu, ohne dass man erkennen würde, wer sich daran zu schaffen macht. Schließlich werden die Konturen eines Mannes erkennbar, der seine ganze Kraft einzusetzen scheint, um die Tür aufzuwuchten und von ihr immer wieder zurückgestoßen wird. Ist es ein freundlicher Besucher oder ein *bad intruder*? Die Tücke des Objekts wird zum Slapstick, ein alltäglicher Vorgang zum ambiguen Spiel zwischen Hoffnung und Horror; das nervöse Gliederzucken der Personen scheint sich wie ein Virus auf die Gegenstände zu übertragen - ein metaphorischer Transfer vom Organischen zum Anorganischen. Ein wenig später bewegt sich der Mann nach vorne. In der Vorwärts-Rückwärts-Doppelbewegung verzerrt sich sein Gesicht zum karnivoren Grinsen, während die Frau freundlich erwartungsvoll lächelt. So entstehen durch die manipulativen Einschreibungen und *time-stretches* emotionale Disproportionalitäten, die das narrative Kontinuum aufbrechen und das Gefühls-Equilibrium, um das sich das Hollywood-Kino *desperately* bemüht, aus der Balance bringen. Die

FLUTTERING

The frame-by-frame method points to a close relationship, invoked by Martin Arnold many times over, with Peter Kubelka and his attempts to capture the unexplored essence of the medium and to decipher the secret messages lurking between the frames. What distinguishes the younger filmmaker, however, is his harking back to the narrative machinery of the classic Hollywood films of the big-studio era. His original material is so charged with references as to inevitably invoke a dialectic of history and the present, of the explicit and the repressed, of the real 'now' and the spooks of the imagination. "Hollywood cinema is a cinema of exclusion, of reduction and denial, a cinema of repression," Arnold told Scott McDonald in a wide-ranging interview. "For this reason we should not only consider what is shown, but also consider what is concealed."

Despite all the formal evolutionary steps in Arnold's cinema work, there are motifs which have nestled, from the beginning of his expedition into the unconscious of cinematic representation, as fluctuating ciphers in the twilight of moving pictures: the eroticism of approach and retreat, the idea of the man-machine, the punishing hand, the nervous fibrillation of neurosis, the shadow of death.

The heroic themes of humanity are not being explicitly exhibited, they tend to, rather, slip in, as it were, in some underhand way, into the mechanics of the strictly regimented course of events. Let us recall *pièce touchée* with its peaceful living room, where a woman is sitting on the sofa, absorbed in her perusal of a magazine. Suddenly a door in the background begins to swing back and forth with a hysterical fluttering motion, yet without the audience being able to identify who is actually causing the trouble. Eventually, the contours of a man can be discerned who appears to be using all of his strength to heave open the door but who is being thrust back by it time and time again. Is he a friendly visitor or some intruder with evil intentions? The treacherous object suggests a slapstick scene, where a simple, day-to-day operation becomes an ambiguous play between hope and horror. The nervous shakes of every limb displayed by the characters seem to infect, like some sort of a virus, even the inanimate objects, as a metaphorical transference from the organic to the inorganic. A little later, the man finally moves forward. In the toing-and-froing dual movement his face is distorted into a carnivorous grin, while the woman smiles with friendly expectation. In this manner, through manipulative inscription and the use of time-stretches, emotional disproportionalities are engendered, which break up the narrative continuity and throw the equilibrium of passions, which the Hollywood cinema desperately strives to achieve, out of kilter.

quälend langsam inszenierte Begegnung öffnet für den Betrachter einen evokativen Raum, der ein Handlungsspektrum des Mannes von zärtlicher Berührung bis zu aggressiver Penetration und sogar physischer Züchtigung plausibel erscheinen lässt. Eine Multiplizität emotionaler Möglichkeiten, auf die die Frau unangemessen eindimensional reagiert.

DOPPELGÄNGER

Die stockende Vorwärtsbewegung des Mannes wird von seinem Schatten begleitet, der in der Kürze des Ablaufs der originalen Einstellung kaum wahrnehmbar ist. In Martin Arnolds Palimpsest jedoch emanzipiert sich der schemenhafte Begleiter zum veritablen Doppelgänger. Weitere ‚imaginäre' Spiegelgestalten entstehen durch die seitenverkehrte Projektion der Kader, die als *trompe l'œuil* -Effekt eine ‚schizoide' Aufspaltung der Figuren bewirken. Hier wird zum ersten Mal im Werk des Filmemachers das Motiv des Unheimlichen getriggert, das wie ein sinistres Fluidum durch die hyperkinetischen Choreographien seines Marionettentheaters geistert. Das seit der Romantik literarisch weit verbreitete Doppelgänger-Motiv wurde ursprünglich als Versicherung gegen den Untergang des Ich gedeutet. Freuds Ich-Theorie jedoch arbeitete den Gegensatz zwischen der kritischen Ich-Instanz und dem unbewusst Verdrängten heraus, das sich im Widergänger manifestiere. In Anlehnung an Ranks Standardtext „Der Doppelgänger" charakterisiert Freud die Spiegelgestalt als ambivalente Erscheinung: Ursprünglich als unsterbliche Seele und Begleiter des Leibes „eine Dementierung des Todes", habe sich der Doppelgänger in eine Zwangsvorstellung verwandelt, in die Wiederkehr des Todes.

Der kaum wahrnehmbare Schatten aus einer peripheren Szene des Films *The Human Jungle* wird somit in Martin Arnolds Remix *pièce touchée* zu einer beklemmenden Präsenz: In seiner durch die Eingriffe des Regisseurs ironisch zugespitzten Mimesis der erratischen Bewegungen des Mannes entfaltet er die penetrative Wucht einer Todesmetapher, wird er zur Verkörperung des Unheimlichen im Sinne Schellings, der bemerkt hat, unheimlich sei alles, was im Verborgenen hätte bleiben sollen und hervorgetreten sei.

Der Tod und das Unheimliche tragen in Arnolds Oeuvre viele Masken: Sie blitzen in dem bedrohlich ausgestreckten Arm Gregory Pecks auf, der in *passage à l'acte* seinen Sohn auf seinen Platz am Frühstücktisch befehligen möchte. Die impertinente Insistenz der Befehlsgeste wird durch Geräusche unterstrichen, die an das Geknatter eines Maschinengewehrs erinnern - ein Trommelfeuer des Grauens.

The painfully slow unfolding of the encounter opens up for the viewer an evocative space, which seems to allow the man a spectrum of plausible actions ranging from tender physical contact to aggressive penetration and even corporal punishment - a multiplicity of emotional potentialities, to which the woman reacts disproportionately mono-dimensional.

DOPPELGÄNGERS

The hesitant forward motion of the man is accompanied by his shadow, which in the brevity of the course of the original sequence was barely noticeable. In Martin Arnold's palimpsest, however, the shadowy companion is emancipated into a veritable *doppelgänger*. Further 'imaginary' characters come into being through the inverted projection of frames, which, in *a trompe l'oeil*-effect cause a 'schizoid' split of the characters to occur. Here, for the first time in the work of this filmmaker, the motif of the uncanny is being triggered, which, like a sinister fluid, moves about, ghostlike, through the hyper-kinetic choreographies of his puppet theatre. The *doppelgänger* motif, common in literature since the Romantic Age, was initially interpreted as a form of insurance against the disintegration of the self. Freud, in his theory of the personality, however, uncovered the contrast between the critical instance of the ego and the unconsciously repressed, which supposedly manifests itself in the return of the revenant. Based on Rank's standard text, *Der Doppelgänger*, Freud characterised the mirror image as an ambivalent appearance: originally as the immortal soul and companion of the body, "a demnetation of death", the *doppelgänger* had been transformed, according to Freud, into an obsession, the recurrence of death.

The barely noticeable shadow from a peripheral scene of the film *The Human Jungle*, thus becomes, in Martin Arnold's remix, *pièce touchée*, a stifling presence. In this pointedly ironic mimesis of the man's erratic movements the director has been able, through his interference with the material, to unfold the penetrative impact of a metaphor for death into an embodiment of the uncanny in the sense of Schelling, who once defined it as anything that should have remained hidden but had come out into the open.

Death and the uncanny wear many masks in Arnold's oeuvre. They flash up in the threateningly stretched-out arm of Gregory Peck, who, in *passage à l'acte* wishes to command his son to take his seat at the breakfast table. The impertinent insistence of the commanding gesture is underlined by sound effects reminiscent of the crackle of a machine gun, a barrage of dread.

SPRACHZERFALL

Unheimlich ist auch die Behandlung der Sprache im gleichen Film: Die Artikulationen sind in einem prä-(oder post?)semantischen Feld zwischen sinnentleerter Lautproduktion und qualvollen Verbalisierungsversuchen situiert. Einfache Worte und Floskeln wie „Come on" oder „Sister" verketten sich zu repetitiven Stakkati, andere degenerieren zu inintelligiblem Stammeln, Röcheln oder Schreien. Das erinnert an die avancierten Techniken des *turntablism* im Hip Hop, wo durch das Vor- und Zurückbewegen einer Platte ähnliche Effekte erzielt werden. Aus diesem Grund nehmen wir *passage à l'acte* ganz anders wahr als *pièce touchée*: Während im Debüt die Tonspur einen bedrohlichen Grund- *Drone* formuliert und stoisch neben den visuellen Exuberanzen eines zum Tanzen gebrachten Wohnzimmers und seiner Bewohner herläuft, so hat *passage à l'acte* einen Beat: Im Soundgewitter von knallenden Türen und hämmerndem Besteck fühlt sich der Betrachter „aufgeladen und beschleunigt wie ein Partikel /.../ ein Ding." (Ulrich Raulff) Er ist bereit, sich vom Rhythmus tragen zu lassen und er nimmt gleichzeitig am Drama eines Sprachzerfalls teil, das wahlweise als Zertrümmerung der Semantik und damit der gutgeölten Hollywood-Erzählmaschine gedeutet werden kann oder aber als intentionale Regression in eine primordiale Zone jenseits der Befehlsketten einer Idiomatik, die als normative Setzung im Filmdialog die gesellschaftliche Kommunikation dirigiert. In Martin Arnolds Film gelingt im Gesang der Familie im Feuerofen eine Epiphanie, wie sie Roland Barthes in „Die Rauheit der Stimme" am Beispiel eines russischen Basses beschrieben hat: „Etwas ist da, unüberhörbar und eigensinnig (man hört nur es), was jenseits (oder diesseits) der Bedeutung der Wörter liegt, ihrer Form, der Koloratur und selbst des Vortragsstils: etwas, was direkt der Körper des Sängers ist, /.../ als spannte sich über das innere Fleisch des Vortragenden und über die von ihm gesungene Musik ein und dieselbe Haut."

Während in *passage à l'acte* die *Grand Guignol* - Attitüde der Inszenierung das sinistre Thema vom Zerfall der Sprache und damit der Welt überlagert, so wird in *Alone* die Rauheit der Stimme als kubistisches Melodram ausgefaltet: Die zu einem Netz der Bedeutungsvieldimensionalitäten verwobenen Mikro-Erzählungen der ersten beiden Filme verengen sich hier zu einem durchaus monokausal lesbaren narrativen Strang, der von einigen Interpreten als ödipale Tragödie interpretiert worden ist: Es geht um eine komplexe Annäherung zweier jugendlicher Liebender (Mickey Rooney, Judy Garland), um eine begehrte Mutter und einen strafenden Vater.

LANGUAGE DISINTEGRATION

Uncanny, too, is the treatment of language in the same film. All articulations have been arranged on a pre- (or post-?) semantic scale, ranging from utterances devoid of any sense to agonising attempts at verbalisation. Simple words and set phrases, such as "come on" or "sister" are chained together into repetitive staccatos, while others degenerate into unintelligible gibberish, throaty death rattles or shouts. This is reminiscent of the advanced techniques of *turntablism* in hip hop, where similar effects are produced by the forward and backward rotation of a record. For this reason, we perceive *passage à l'acte* entirely differently from *pièce touchée*. For while in the debut film the sound-track formulates a threating basic drone that stoically runs alongside the visual exuberances of a living room that, together with its inhabitants, has been made to dance, *passage à l'acte*, by contrast, has a beat. In the sonic thunderstorm of banging doors and hammering cutlery, the viewer feels "charged and speeded-up like a particle/.../ a thing." (Ulrich Raulff.) Ready and willing to be carried off by the rhythm, the viewer simultaneously participates in the drama of linguistic disintegration, which can be interpreted, according to taste or preference, as either a demolition of semantics and, along with it, the well-oiled Hollywood narrative machinery, or yet as an intentional regression into a primordial zone beyond the chains of command of an idiomatics, which, as a normative given in the cinematic dialogue, directs all societal communications. In Martin Anold's film the song of the family in the fireplace succeeds in establishing an epiphany of the kind which Roland Barthes in "The Grain of the Voice" has described upon the instance of listening to a Russian bass: "There is something there, manifest and persistent (you only hear that), which is past (or previous to) the meaning of the words, of their form (the litany), of the melisma, and even of the style of the performance: something which is directly the singer's body, /.../ as if a single skin lined the performer's inner flesh and the music he sings."

While in *passage à l'acte* the *grand guignol*-like attitude of the production is superimposed on the sinister theme of the disintegration of language and hence the world, in *Alone* the hoarseness of the voice is unfolded as a Cubist melodrama: the micro-narratives woven into a net of multi-dimensionalities of meaning of the first two films contract here into a narrative strand which may well be read as mono-causal and which has been interpreted by some as an Oedipal tragedy. It is a question of a complex rapprochement between two youthful lovers (Mickey Rooney, Judy Garland) around a coveted mother and a punitive father.

TOD

Man kann diesen Film auf die freizügig offerierte freudianische Matrix auftragen, doch interessanter, als das ohnehin schon Offensichtliche noch einmal zu benennen, ist die Suche nach Spuren, die über das ideologisch eingezäunte Feld hinausweisen. Am interessantesten in *Alone* ist die Judy Garland-Figur, deren Gesang die aus drei verschiedenen Hollywood-Filmen kompilierte 15-minütige Arbeit zusammenhält. Auch diese Stimme erleben wir, ähnlich wie in *passage à l'acte* im Vor- und Rücklauf. Statt der fast perkussiven Vokal-Stakkati des älteren Films hören wir nun aber neben Meta-Jodlern, die aus granularen Sound-Partikeln kondensiert wurden, tatsächlich Melodien oder zumindest Melodiefragmente. Auch Judy Garland artikuliert sich vorwiegend in einer prä- (oder post-) zivilisatorischen Sprache der Verstümmelung, doch anders als in *passage à l'acte* entweichen ihr ein paar deutlich prononcierte Worte: „On a night that was meant for love" ist da zu hören oder, besonders klar konturiert, „Alone", der Titel des Films.

In der satanistischen Rockmusik gibt es eine Technik, die es ermöglichen soll, geheime Botschaften skandalösen Inhalts unerkannt an die Adressaten zu versenden: das sogenannte *backwards masking*. Spielt man eine Platte auf reguläre Weise ab, so ist nur sinnloses Gestammel zu hören. Läuft der Tonträger jedoch rückwärts, so enthüllt sich das Kryptogramm in seiner semantischen Dimension. Ähnlich funktioniert die Tonspur des Filmes von Martin Arnold: Buchstabieren wir das Wort *Alone* von hinten nach vorne, so entsteht die Lautfolge Enola im zum idiotischen Grinsen verzerrten Mund Judy Garlands. *Enola* Gay wiederum war der Name jener Fliegenden Festung B-29, mit der Squadron Commander Paul W. Tibbets am 6. August 1945 nach Japan aufbrach, um die Atombombe über Hiroshima abzuwerfen. Auf einer Website zu dieser militärischen Mission findet man den Satz: „Wie die meisten Flugzeuge in der Army hatte auch dieses einen Spitznamen: Tibbets nannte es, zur Ehre seiner Mutter, Enola Gay und ließ diesen Namen direkt vor dem Abflug auf beide Seiten der Maschine malen."

Somit scheint in *Alone* die selbstevidente Figuren-Konstellation nur zu verschleiern, dass es um etwas ganz Anderes geht: Um eine aus dem Hohlraum der Geschichte gefilterte mega/meta-ödipale Metapher der Zerstörung, die das Begehren kontaminiert hat; um eine fundamentale Befragung von Lebens- und Todestrieben und ein existentielles Taumeln unter dem Diktat von Wiederholungszwängen. Das Satyrspiel um Mickey und Judy, Mutter und Vater verdeckt eine fundamentale Wahrheit, die in *Alone* ausgesprochen wird: Liebe ist kälter als der Tod.

DEATH

One may paste this film onto the liberally-offered Freudian matrix, but more interesting than reiterating again what is already abundantly obvious is the search for traces pointing beyond the ideologically fenced-in terrain. The most interesting figure in *Alone* is the Judy Garland character, whose singing brackets the 15-minute work compiled from three separate Hollywood films. Again we experience, as in *passage à l'acte*, her voice in a back-and-forth run. Instead of the almost percussive vocal staccatos of the earlier film, however, we now hear, besides meta-yodels condensed from granular sound particles, actual melodies or at least melodic fragments. Judy Garland, too, displays a preference for articulating a pre- (or post-) civilisational language of mutilations, but unlike *passage à l'acte* she occasionally lets fly with some clearly enunciated words. "On a night that was meant for love", she can be heard to say, and, in particularly clear outline, "Alone", the film's title.

In satanic rock music there exists a technique called backwards masking, which is supposed to render it possible to send, undetected, secret messages of a scandalous nature to its intended audience. If a record is played in the regular way, all that can be heard will be a meaningless stammer. If the sound recording is played backwards, the cryptogram reveals itself within a comprehensible semantic dimension. The sonic track of Martin Arnold's film functions in a similar way. If we spell the word *Alone* back-to-front, a sequence of sounds comprising the word *Enola* appears in Judy Garland's idiotically-grinning, distorted mouth. Enola Gay, in turn, was the name of that Flying Fortress, the B-29, in which squadron commander Paul W. Tibbets on the morning of August 6, 1945, set out for Japan to drop the atomic bomb over Hiroshima. In a website covering this military mission, the following piece of information can be found: "Like most aeroplanes in the army, this one too had a nickname. Tibbets called it Enola Gay, in honour of his mother, and had the name painted on both sides of his plane just before take-off."

So it would appear that in *Alone* the self-evident constellation of characters merely veils the fact that something totally different is at issue. The real issue is a mega/meta-Oedipal metaphor for destruction, filtered from the cavernous hollow of history, which has contaminated all desire; it is a matter of a fundamental querying of the drives dominating life and death and an existential stagger under the dictates of compulsive repetitions. The satyriac game involving Mickey and Judy, mother and father, covers up the fundamental truth enunciated in *Alone*: that Love is colder than Death.

MENSCH-MASCHINE

Deanimated bringt die Motive vom Zerfall der Sprache und vom letalen Ausstieg zu einer logischen Conclusio: Zwar sind noch vereinzelte Dialogpartikel wie Ruinen einer lückenlosen Kommunikation in die Tonspur eingegraben, doch über weite Strecken des Films stehen einander Personen mit zugemorphten Mündern gegenüber, die ratlos vor sich hinstarren. Erst in dieser Dialektik aus artikulatorischen Schwundstufen und dem endgültigen Verstummen breitet sich jene unendliche Leere aus, die für den Film kennzeichnend ist. Der Tod, der wie eine Halluzination durch die ersten drei Filme Martin Arnolds oszilliert, wird in *Deanimated* zu jener Furie des Verschwindens, die von einem „unerträglichen Hinausgehen über das Dasein" (Georges Bataille) kündet. Die Ekstase der Vernichtung, die Annihilierung des Seins, die Hypostasierung des Anorganischen, der suchende Blick, der nicht mehr auf das Erkennen trifft, sind jene Relais, die den Übergang zur katatonischen Starre vorbereiten.

Der Wahnsinn, den die Ungeheuerlichkeit des Nichts provoziert, ist in die Gesichter eingeschrieben: Das belustigte Lächeln des schwarzen Dieners, der einem leeren Stuhl serviert, die hilflose Mimik des Liebespaares, das keine Worte findet, um die intime Situation verbal zu möblieren. Im angeekelten Augenrollen, in der Verkrampfung der Gesichtsmuskeln dieser beiden Figuren sind letzte Spuren jener nervösen Tics abgebildet, die in Arnolds ersten Filmen die Kinetik der Abläufe bestimmten.

Durch die Zergliederung und Rekombination der propulsiven Bewegungen verwandeln sich die Schauspieler in *pièce touchée, passage à l'acte* und *Alone* in eigenartig androide Erscheinungen: Das unmotivierte Gliederzucken, Kopfwerfen, Grimassieren und Stottern mag auf einen psychischen Defekt im Sinne des Tourette-Syndroms verweisen („Multiple motorische Tics sowie mindestens ein vokaler Tic treten im Verlauf der Krankheit auf, jedoch nicht unbedingt gleichzeitig"; Michael Wittmann) oder aber bereits eine Transgression der existentiellen Verfasstheit signalisieren: Seit La Mettrie 1748 in *L`homme machine* dem Menschen den Status eines komplexen Apparates zugesprochen hat, ist die Idee von der Mensch-Maschine eine gleichermaßen angstauslösende wie erregende Vorstellung. Der Mythos vom Cyborg evoziert einen Triumph des Intellekts, lässt völlig neue Amalgame zwischen dem organischen Sein und seinen technologischen Extensionen möglich erscheinen, signifiziert aber gleichzeitig ein postsozietäres Zeitalter der rein virtuellen Konnexionen, in dem der Mensch überflüssig geworden ist. Eine Epoche, wie sie in den leeren Zimmerfluchten und kommunikativen Leerstellen von *Deanimated* bereits metaphorisch antizipiert zu sein scheint. „Vielleicht gibt es eine Maschine", schreibt Thomas Pynchon in

THE MAN-MACHINE

Deanimated takes the motifs of the disintegration of language and the lethal bale-out to a logical conclusion. It is true, some singular particles of dialogue may still be buried, like the ruins of a once immaculate communication, within the soundtrack, but across broad stretches of the film people, with their mouths morphed shut, keep staring at one another, utterly at a loss. It is only in this dialectic of a gradual decrease of articulation and the eventual loss of speech that an infinite emptiness unfolds as the film's characteristic hallmark. Death, which oscillates like a hallucination through Martin Arnold's first three films, becomes, in *Deanimated*, that fury of disapperance which gives witness to an "unbearable transition beyond existence" (Georges Bataille). The ecstasy of extermination, the annihilation of being, the hypostatisation of the inorganic, the searching glance, which no longer meets with any species of recognition, those are the relays which prepare the transition to a catatonic rigidity.

The madness provoked by the enormity of the void has been incribed into the faces, into the amused smile of the black servant, who waits upon an empty chair, into the facial expressions of the lovers unable to find words to provide the verbal furniture for the intimate situation. In the disgusted rolling of the eyes, the cramping of the facial muscles of these two characters there can be seen the final traces of those nervous tics, which determined the kinetics of the course of events in Arnold's first few films.

By dint of the disintegration and recombination of their propulsive movements the actors in *pièce touchée, passage à l'acte* and *Alone* transform into curiously androidal appearances. The unmotivated jerking of limbs, tossing of head, grimassing and stuttering may point to a defect along the lines of Tourette's Syndrome ("multiple motoric tics as well as at least one vocal tic make their appearances during the course of the illness, although not necessarily all at the same time", according to Michael Wittmann) - or they may already signal a transgression of the existential state of mind. Since La Mettrie in 1748 in his *L'homme machine* ascribed to man the status of a complex apparatus, the idea of the man-machine has been an equally fear-inducing and exciting concept. The myth of the cyborg evokes a triumph of the intellect, allowing completely new amalgams between the organic being and its technological extensions to appear possible, yet simultaneously signalling a post-societary era of purely virtual connections where human beings will have become superfluous. An epoch of a sort that appears, in the vacant flight of rooms and the communicative voids of *Deanimated*, to have been already metaphorically anticipated. "M-maybe there is a machine," as Thomas Pynchon has written in *Gravity's Rainbow*, " to take us away, take us completely,

Gravity's Rainbow, „die uns von hier wegnimmt, die uns ganz zu sich nimmt, uns durch die Elektroden auf dem Schädel in sich einsaugt, damit wir auf ewig in der Maschine leben, zusammen mit den anderen Seelen, die sie in sich gespeichert hat."

Die Faszination der devianten Entitäten, die Martin Arnolds Filme bevölkern (oder neuerdings: entvölkern) liegt gerade in der Ambiguität ihrer ontologischen Bestimmung: Man mag im spastischen Rütteln von Gregory Peck in *passage à l'acte* oder im inhibierten gesanglichen Liebeswerben von Judy Garland in *Alone* Elemente jenes guten Irren sehen wollen, der in der Schizo-Theorie von Deleuze/Guattari zum Träger aller verbotenen Wünsche und archaisch andrängenden Subversionslüste wird. Oder man erkennt in dem scheinbar nicht zielgerichteten, von repetitiven Pulsionen erschütterten Wirken der Figuren den Geist jenes *merveilleux mécanique* (Michel Carrouges), das jenseits der kartesianischen Körper-/Geist-Dichotomie ein schrecklich-wunderbares Paralleluniversum aufspannt.

Martin Arnolds Filme sind gnadenlose Investigationen von Geschichte und Gegenwart. Sie versuchen in dem durch historische Distanz fremd Gewordenen das Eigene zu finden und es wiederum in ein Anderes zu wenden. Sie stellen die fundamentale Frage nach dem Wesen des Menschen und der Dinge in der technischen Welt, die, nach Heidegger, „äußerste Transparenz und zugleich tiefste Obskurität" verkörpert.

suck us through the electrodes out of the skull 'n' into the Machine and live there forever with all the other souls it's got stored there."

The fascination whith the deviant entities that populate Martin Arnold's films (or more recently: that depopulate them) lies precisely in the ambiguity of their ontological determination. One may wish to see in the spastic shakes of Gregory Peck in *passage à l'acte* or in the inhibited cantatorial wooing of Judy Garland in *Alone* certain elements of the good lunatic who has become in Deleuze/Guatari's schizo-theory the carrier of all prohibited desires and archaic onslaughts of subversive desires. Or else one may recognise in the seemingly non-goal-directed actions of the protagonists, shattered by repetitive impulses, the spirit of that marvelous mechanic (Michel Carrouges) who, beyond the Cartesian body-and-mind dichotomy sets up a terrible and wonderful parallel universe.

Martin Arnold's films are merciless investigations of the historic and the present. They attempt to find within what has become strange through historical distance something of our own and to turn it into something else again. They ask that fundamental question regarding the nature of man and all things within a technological world which, according to Heidegger, embodies "utter transparency and, at the same time, the deepest obscurity".

*

Good night, dad.

*   *

. . . . — . . . .

Good night.

*   *   *   *

·   ·   ·   ·   ·   ·   ·   ·   ·   ·   l   ·   ·   ·   ·   ·   l   ·   ·   ·   ·   ·   ·   ·   ·   l   ·   ·   ·   l

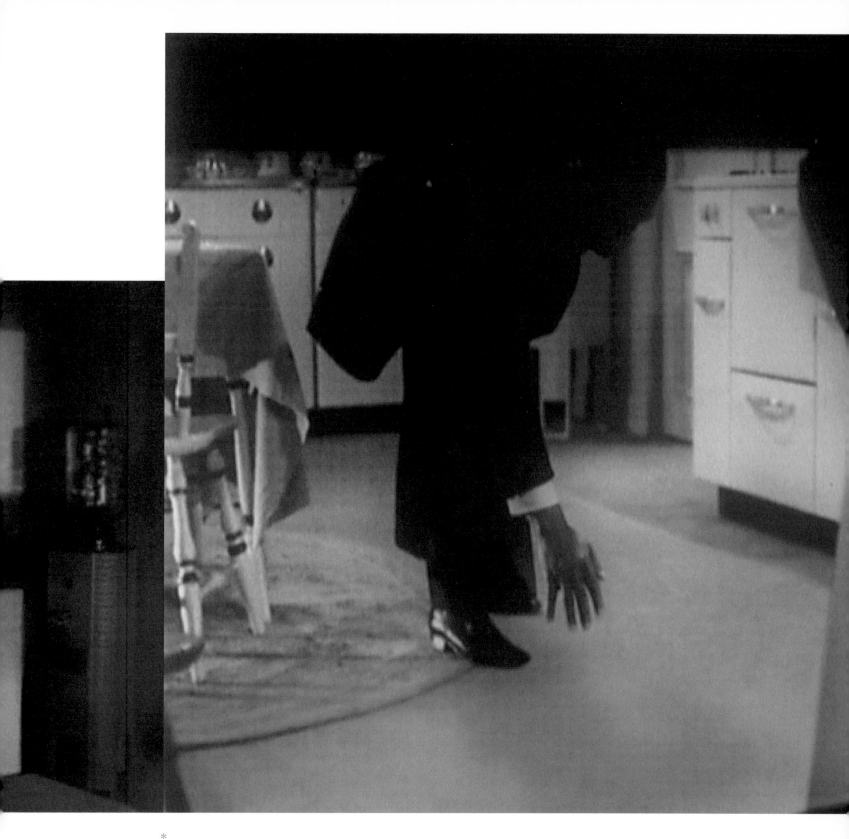

Hello, operator.

No. Yes. All right.

Good morning, Evans.

Now, what's the matter?

What?

Well, I guess that's that.

No clues, no fingerprints, no motive, nothing.

Hmmm!

*

*

Hello there.

*

Akira Mizuta Lippit

Akira Mizuta Lippit

Kinematographie. In einem kurzen Aufsatz aus dem Jahr 1973, *L'Acinéma*, spekuliert Jean-François Lyotard über die Beziehung zwischen Kino und Verneinung, das Filmemachen als Werk des Verneinens von Bewegung.[1] Der Titel des Essays formt beinahe ein Wortspiel, ein abgebrochenes Wortspiel, eine stille Verneinung der Verneinung, eine Denegation von „la cinéma" als „l'acinéma". Nur, dass im Französischen das Wort „cinéma" den männlichen Artikel trägt, „le cinéma". Lyotards Negation von Cinéma als *Acinéma* bewirkt ein leises, fast unhörbares Nachrauschen durch die ohnehin schon etwas geschwächte Akustik der mit einem Geschlechtsartikel versehenen Nomina. „La cinéma", „l'acinéma" stellt ein geschlechtlich umgewandeltes Kino dar (die Verneinung des Kinos durch seine Feminisierung); Lyotards „a", welches die Basis seiner Verneinung bildet, transponiert das eine Kino in den Körper eines anderen, virtuellen Kinos: des *acinéma*, des Kinos der Eliminierungen. Es ist eine Form des Kinos unter vielen möglichen Kinoformen, *a cinema*, aber auch die Antithese zum Kino, *anti-cinema*, Acinéma. Dies ist das andere oder Nicht-Kino, in einem Frauenkörper, eine Art Drag-Kino. Eine **M**utter des Kinos.

In *L'Acinéma* besteht Lyotard darauf, dass, obwohl „Kinematographie das Einschreiben von Bewegung" ist, individuelle Filme durch die Beseitigung überflüssiger Bewegungen von „Schauspielern und anderen bewegten Objekten", aber auch von „Lichtern, Farben, Rahmen und Linse"[2] entstünden. „Es scheint", sagt er, „dass sich Bild, Sequenz und der ganze Film um den Preis dieser Ausschlüsse konstituieren müssen."[3] Ein jeder Film wird geschaffen, indem einige Bewegungen erhalten und andere eliminiert werden. „*Welche* Bewegungen und sich bewegenden Körper [*mobiles*] sind dies? Warum ist es notwendig, unter ihnen auszuwählen, auszusortieren und sie auszuschließen?"[4]

Lyotards Beschreibung impliziert ein Gleichgewicht zwischen der Einschreibung von Bewegung und ihrer Beseitigung, zwischen Inskription und Exskription. Ein angemessener Grad an Ausschlüssen produziert eine Ordnung der Bewegung. Einen synthetischen Körper von Bewegungen, dazu geschaffen, organisch zu erscheinen. Einen Film-**Korpus**. Jede einzelne Bewegung stellt eine eigene, besondere Kraft dar, das, was Lyotard eine „Intensität" nennt, die entweder zur Ordnung des Ganzen beiträgt oder droht, den Film auseinander zu reißen, seinen narrativen Bogen in sich zusammenbrechen zu lassen. Fehlgeleitete Bewegungen werden eliminiert, samt ihren Intensitäten, bis der Film einem Ordnungsgefüge zu ähneln beginnt, einem organischen Korpus.

„Wir stellen fest, dass das Hervorstechende [le *décrochage*] wegen seiner Abweichung beseitigt wird, um also eine Ordnung des Ganzen (der Aufnahme und/oder der Sequenz und/oder des Films) zu wahren und zugleich die Intensität, die es befördert, zu verbieten. Und die Ordnung des Ganzen hat ihren Grund einzig

Cinematography. In a brief essay from 1973, *L'Acinéma*, Jean-François Lyotard speculates on the relation between cinema and negation, filmmaking as the labor of negating movement.[1] The title of the essay almost forms a pun, forms an almost or aborted pun, a silent negation of the negation, a denegation of "la cinéma" as l'acinéma." Only the French word "cinéma" carries a masculine article, "le cinéma." Lyotard's negation of cinema as acinema produces a mild sonic play, almost inaudible, through the already somewhat faint acoustics of gendered nouns. "La cinéma," "l'acinéma" represents a transgendered cinema (the negation of cinema as feminization); Lyotard's "a," which forms the basis of the negation, transposes one cinema into the body of another, virtual cinema, *acinema* of eliminations. One cinema among many possible cinemas, *a cinema*, but also the antithesis of cinema, anti-cinema, acinema. The other or non-cinema in a woman's body, as a woman's body, a kind of drag cinema. A **m**other cinema.

In *L'Acinéma*, Lyotard insists that although "cinematography is the inscription of movement," individual films are created by eliminating the superfluous movements of "actors and other moving objects," but also "of lights, colors, frame, and lens."[2] "It seems," he says, "that image, sequence, and film must be constituted at the price of these exclusions."[3] Each film is formed by retaining some movements and eliminating others. "*Which* movements and moving bodies [*mobiles*] are these? Why is it necessary to select, sort out, and exclude them?"[4]

Lyotard's description implies a balance between the inscription of movement and its elimination, between inscription and exscription. An appropriate level of excision produces an order of movement. A synthetic body of movements, designed to appear organic. A film **corpus**. Each movement represents a specific force, what Lyotard calls an "intensity," which either contributes to the order of the whole or threatens to pull the film apart, to disorganize its narrative or trajectory. Mistaken movements are eliminated, along with their intensities, until the film comes to resemble an order, an organic corpus.

"We observe that if the mistake [*le décrochage*] is eliminated it is because of its incongruity, and to protect the order of the whole (shot and/or sequence and/or film) while banning the intensity it carries. And the order of the whole has its sole object in the functioning of the cinema: that there be order in the movements, that movements be made in order, that they make order. Writing with movements - cinematography - is thus conceived and practiced as an incessant organizing of movements following the rules of representation for spatial localization, those of narration for the instantiation of language, and those of the form "film music" for the sound track. The so-called impression of reality is a real oppression of orders."[5]

und allein in der Funktionsfähigkeit des Kinos: es muss Ordnung in den Bewegungen herrschen, die Bewegungen müssen einer Ordnung folgen, sie müssen in Ordnung sein. Mit Bewegungen zu schreiben – Kinematographieren – wird als stete Organisation von Bewegung aufgefasst und dementsprechend gehandhabt. Es gibt Regeln der Repräsentation für die Lokalisierung im Raum, Regeln der Narrration für die Strukturierung der Sprache, Regeln des Genres „Filmmusik" für die Tonspur. Der sogenannte Realitätseindruck ist in Wirklichkeit ein Ordnungszwang."[5]

Die Organisation von Bewegungen beinhaltet die Beseitigung von verstreuten Intensitäten, „die Unterordnung aller Partialtriebe, aller sterilen und abweichenden Bewegungen", bis zuletzt eine Ordnung sichtbar, ja sogar spürbar wird.[6] Dieser Korpus aus Bewegungen, aus Kinematographien, bestimmt das Gesetz eines jeden einzelnen Films, geordnet und organisch, geboren aus einem „Nihilismus der Bewegungen"[7]. „Der Film", sagt Lyotard, „ist der organische Körper kinematographischer Bewegungen."[8]

Doch was ist mit den verstreuten Intensitäten? Was geschieht, wenn aus Versehen die richtigen Bewegungen und ihre Intensitäten beseitigt werden und stattdessen die falschen übrig bleiben, um nun durch den Film zu kreisen? Was ist, wenn zu viele Bewegungen eliminiert werden und den Film lethargisch und müde, unbeweglich und leer zurücklassen? **Chaos** oder **Katalepsie**? Überfluss und Mangel an Intensitäten, die zwei Pole von „Bewegungslosigkeit und Bewegungsexzess", dienen, Lyotards Modell zufolge, als die unabdingbare Grundlage für die Möglichkeit von Lust.[9] Für die Möglichkeit einer Investition ohne Gewinn. In der Praxis sind Bewegungslosigkeit und Bewegungsexzess, wie Lyotard anmerkt, Merkmale „des experimentellen und des Underground-Kinos".

Ein Filmemacher, im Besonderen, hat eine ganz eigene Filmkunst aus einem Zuviel oder Zuwenig an Bewegung entwickelt, aus graduellen Unterschieden von Übermaß und Abwesenheit, die in seinem gesamten Filmschaffen eine Serie von Erschütterungen und nervösen Störungen produzieren. In seiner Found Footage Trilogie - *pièce touchée* (1989), *passage à l'acte* (1993), *Alone. Life Wastes Andy Hardy* (1998) - manipuliert Martin Arnold einzelne Filmkader aus verschiedenen Hollywoodfilmen in Schwarzweiß, bricht einzelne Einstellungen, Sequenzen und ganze Szenen im Vibrieren kleiner Exzesse und Absenzen auf. Arnolds *Deanimated: The Invisible Ghost* (2002), basierend auf Joseph H. Lewis' *The Invisible Ghost* (1941), ist eine digitale Bearbeitung des Originals in Spielfilmlänge, die eine Architektur des Kinos entwickelt, welche für Lyotard unvorstellbar war. Unvorgestellt und unvorstellbar innerhalb der Begriffe, die Lyotards Ökonomie definieren, aber auch eine unvorstellbare Art des Kinos an sich. Als Kino des Unvorgestellten und Unvorstellbaren besteht Arnolds

The organization of movements involves the elimination of stray intensities, "the subordination of all partial drives, all sterile and divergent movements," until an order becomes visible, even sensible.[6] This corpus of movements, of cinematographics, determines the law of each individual film, ordered and organic, born from a "nihilism of movements."[7] "The film," says Lyotard, "is the organic body of cinematographic movements."[8]

But what of the stray intensities? What happens when the right movements and their intensities are accidentally eliminated, and the wrong ones left to surge through a film? What if too many movements are eliminated, leaving the film lethargic and tired, immobile and empty? **Chaos** or **catalepsy**? Surplus and deficit intensity, the two poles of "immobility and excess movement," serve, according to Lyotard's schema, as the very basis for the possibility of pleasure.[9] For the possibility of an expenditure without return. In practice, immobility and excess movement are features of, Lyotard notes, the "experimental and underground" cinemas.

One filmmaker in particular, has based an entire cinema on surplus and deficit movement, small degrees of excess and absence that generate throughout his corpus a series of tremors and nervous disorders. In his found footage trilogy, *pièce touchée* (1989), *passage à l'acte* (1993), *Alone. Life Wastes Andy Hardy* (1998), Martin Arnold manipulates individual film frames from various b/w Hollywood films, breaking down shots, sequences, and entire scenes in the vibration of small excesses and absences. Arnold's *Deanimated: The Invisible Ghost* (2002), based on Joseph H. Lewis's *The Invisible Ghost* (1941), is a feature-length digital reworking of the original that develops an architecture of cinema unimagined by Lyotard. Unimagined and unimaginable in the terms that bind Lyotard's economy, but also an unimaginable cinema as such. A cinema of the unimagined and unimaginable, Arnold's work consists of a series of unimages, animages. The *animagination* of cinema in *Deanimated* is not simply a matter of economy, of avoiding returns, but rather of diminishing movement and representation, a materiality of the empty.

Arnold has digitally erased at various points most of the characters from the film in a quasi-random sequence, leaving behind stretches of vacant space and interaction. He has also removed or altered portions of the dialogue and closed the mouths of several speaking actors. Left behind are largely useless and awkward bodies, the nervous residues of disappearance. The bodies have become traces, excesses; they remain in the film uncomfortably. Especially in those scenes in which Arnold has morphed the mouth of characters shut.[10] During scenes that originally contained dialogue, Arnold has, in places, removed the voices and digitally sutured the actors' mouths shut. The result is a deformed set of

Werk aus einer Reihe von Nicht-Bildern, Antibildern. Die *anima-gination* des Kinos in *Deanimated* ist nicht einfach eine Frage der Ökonomie, des Vermeidens der Wiederkehr, sondern vielmehr einer nachlassenden Bewegung und Darstellung, einer Materialität des Leeren.

Arnold hat an verschiedenen Punkten die meisten Figuren aus dem Film in einer gleichsam zufälligen Reihenfolge digital ausgelöscht und dabei entleerte Raumzonen und stillgelegte Interaktionen zurückgelassen. Darüber hinaus hat er Teile des Dialogs entfernt oder verändert und die Münder von mehreren im Original heftig deklamierenden Schauspielern verschlossen. Zurück bleiben großteils nutzlose und unbeholfene Leiber, nervöse Rückstände des Verschwindens. Die Körper sind zu Spuren geworden, zu Exzessen; sie verbleiben voller Unbehagen im Film - ganz besonders in jenen Szenen, in denen Arnold die Münder der Schauspieler zugemorpht hat.[10] In Szenen, die ursprünglich Dialoge enthalten hatten, entfernte Arnold an bestimmten Stellen die Stimmen und nähte digital die Münder der Schauspieler zu. Das Ergebnis ist eine Assemblage entstellter Körpergesten, die wie impulsgesteuerte Zuckungen und der Versuch ihrer Beherrschung wirken. In Abwesenheit des Dialogs scheinen die Körper die Dauer einer Konversation auszusitzen, mit ängstlichen Blicken auf den jeweils anderen, auf irgendein Zeichen der Erlösung hoffend.

In einer frühen Szene des Films speist Kessler (Bela Lugosi) mit seiner Frau, die für die anderen Figuren - ebenso wie für das Publikum - unsichtbar ist. (Mrs. Kessler ist, wie man vermutet, gestorben, und der Witwer leidet jedes Jahr an dem melancholischen Irrglauben, sie lebe mit ihm noch so wie früher. Sie ist tatsächlich noch am Leben, aber wahnsinnig geworden, und erteilt ihrem Mann den Befehl zum Morden.) Einzig Kessler sieht seine imaginäre Frau. Evans, der Butler, und Virginia, seine Tochter, machen gute Miene zum bösen Spiel. Als Virginias Liebhaber, Ralph, zufällig auftaucht, zieht ihn Virginia zur Seite, um ihm die Situation zu erklären. An diesem Punkt streicht Arnold Teile aus den Dialogen und fügt dafür eine Reihe von digitalen Morphs in das Gespräch ein. „Ich verstehe nicht" ... „Nun, es passierte vor einigen Jahren" ... „Vater verehrte mich" („verehrte sie", im Original) ... „Es brach meinem Vater fast das Herz". Während der gesamten Szene sorgen unpassende Gesten, unmotivierte Blicke und aggressiv aufgeladene Schweigephasen oder verweigerte Antworten für einen leicht hysterisch wirkenden Zusammenbruch der beiden. (Durch die Änderung in Virginias Erklärungen, den Wechsel von Kesslers Zuneigung von „ihr", seiner Frau - zu „mir" - Virginia, führt Arnold das Thema des Inzests in *Deanimated* ein, das, als Subtext, den gesamten Film durchzieht.) Plötzlich stürzt Ralph auf Virginia zu und beginnt, sie leidenschaftlich zu küssen.

bodily gestures that seem like impulsive twitches and attempted restraint. Absent the dialogue, the bodies seem to wait out the duration of the conversation, anxiously gazing at the other for any sign of relief.

Early in the film, Kessler (Bela Lugosi) dines with his wife, who is invisible to the other characters as well as the audience. (Mrs. Kessler is presumed dead and the widower suffers each year from a melancholic delusion. She is in fact alive and mad, and commands her husband to murder.) Only Kessler sees his imaginary wife. Evans, the butler, and Virginia, his daughter, play along with the charade. When Virginia's boyfriend Ralph stumbles on the scene, Virginia pulls him aside to explain the situation. At this point, Arnold introduces a series of vocal lapses and digital morphs into their conversation. "I don't understand" ... "Well it happened several years ago" ... "Father worshipped me" ("worshipped her," in the original)... "It almost broke my father's heart." Throughout the scene, inappropriate gestures, unmotivated looks, and aggressive silences or non-responses generate a mildly hysterical breakdown between the two. (By changing, in Virginia's explanation, the object of Kessler's affection from "her" - his wife - to "me" - Virginia, Arnold has initiated the theme of incest, which remains as a subtext throughout *Deanimated*.) Suddenly, Ralph lunges toward Virginia and begins to kiss her passionately. Nothing has been explained, nothing has provoked the embrace, which appears driven by an inexplicable libidinal surge. (One objective of the commercial cinema, says Lyotard, is to purge "*all impulsional movement*" [*tout mouvement impulsionnel*].")[11] The scene ends when the camera cuts to a close-up of Ralph, who looks startled, as if discovered in the act of committing a crime. He looks toward the foyer and sees Cecile, the maid. His apparent fear, banal and overwrought in the original, is left unexplained in *Deanimated*.

Another feature of *Deanimated* is the insertion of alien technologies into the space of the cinema technique. Once considered the exemplary technology, cinema, in Arnold's revision, looks distantly photographic, faded, pre-technological; the visible horizon constricted and stifling. Arnold has infected the liminal space with a set of barely perceptible technological functions and effects that make Kessler's home, where the film is set, uncanny. Erasures and morphs, which constitute Arnold's principal interventions, tear small movements into and away from the original, recalibrating it as a set of partial intensities. The digital compositing generates visible and invisible meshes in which images are added to and blocked by others.

The returns of each movement, what Lyotard calls "value," have been stripped from the film. The economy of Arnold's cinema generates invaluable, valueless movement. Camera movements with no apparent destination or purpose; zooms and pans to and

Nichts ist erklärt worden, nichts hat die Umarmung herausgefordert, welche von einer unerklärlichen libidinösen Aufwallung angetrieben zu sein scheint. (Ein Ziel des kommerziellen Films, meint Lyotard, sei es, „alle impulsiven Bewegungen" [tout mouvement impulsionel] auszumerzen.)[11] Die Szene endet damit, dass die Kamera zu einer Nahaufnahme auf Ralph ansetzt, der erschrocken aussieht, als wäre er bei einem Verbrechen ertappt worden. Er blickt zur Eingangshalle und sieht Cecile, das Zimmermädchen. Seine offensichtliche Angst, im Original banal und übertrieben, bleibt in Deanimated vollends unerklärlich.

Ein weiteres Merkmal von Deanimated ist der Einsatz von neuen Technologien im Bereich der Filmtechnik. Das Medium Film, das einst als Mustertechnologie galt, sieht in Arnolds Bearbeitung bloß entfernt fotografisch, verwaschen, geradezu vor-technisch aus; der sichtbare Horizont wirkt eingeschränkt und beklemmend. Arnold hat diesen filmischen Raum mit einer Reihe kaum wahrnehmbarer digitaler Effekte infiziert, die Kesslers Haus, den Ort des Geschehens, unheimlich erscheinen lassen. Auslöschungen und Morphs, Arnolds wichtigste Eingriffe, reißen kleine Bewegungen aus dem Original heraus oder setzen sie ein, re-kalibrieren es als ein Set partialer Intensitäten. Das Digital Compositing produziert sichtbare und unsichtbare Geflechte, in denen Bilder hinzugefügt oder durch andere verdeckt werden.

Der Ertrag jeder Bewegung, das, was Lyotard „Wert" nennt, wurde dem Film genommen. Die Ökonomie des Arnoldschen Filmschaffens erzeugt unschätzbare und gleichzeitig wertlose Bewegung. Kamerafahrten ohne ersichtliches Ziel, ohne Zweck, Schwenks und Zooms, die im Nirgendwo enden. Von Zeit zu Zeit ist man überrascht, am Ende einer Kamerafahrt tatsächlich ein Gesicht oder eine Gestalt anzutreffen, als ob die Anwesenheit eines Gesichts oder der Ursprung eines Blicks überflüssig, lächerlich oder anstößig wären. Was treibt dieser Mensch hier in diesem Haus? Der Körper ist selbst ein Zuviel an Bewegung in Arnolds de-animierter Ökonomie, die Schauspieler sind, wie er sagt, **„verkrüppelt"**. Da Schlüsselelemente ihres Körpers - Organe und Stimmen - fehlen, erscheinen sie als nutzlose Assemblagen körperloser Organe. „Auch sie sollen wie Objekte erscheinen", sagt Arnold, „wie das Mobiliar der menschenleeren Innenräume."[12]

Inskription. Eingeschrieben in Deanimated ist eine Form von Phantomtext, eine gespenstische Partitur, ein Schreiben, das das Zeichen entfernt und nur Spuren hinterlässt. De-Skription könnte man dazu sagen, ein Ent-Schreiben, ein Aus-Schreiben, ein Aus-dem-Blickfeld-Schreiben, ein Schreiben, dass nichts als eine grafische Leere hinterlässt: Akinematographie, Schreiben als Beseitigen, Entfernen, Entfernung. **Unsichtbarkeit.** Die Unsichtbarkeit, die Deanimated durchzieht, ist als Störung gekennzeichnet: viele Darsteller scheinen das Ausgelöschte weiter sehen zu können.

from nothing. From time to time, one is surprised to find a face or a figure at the other end of a camera movement, as if the presence of a face, or the origin of a look is gratuitous, ridiculous, or repulsive. What is this person doing there, in the house? The body is itself an excess movement in the de-animated economy of Arnold's work, the actors **"crippled,"** says Arnold. Lacking key elements of their bodies - organs and voices - they are a useless assemblage of organs without bodies. "They should seem to be objects as well," says Arnold, "like the objects in the empty interiors."[12]

Inscription. Inscribed in Deanimated is a form of phantom writing, a ghost script, a writing that removes the sign and leaves only traces. Description, one could say, unscribing, exscribing, writing out of view, a writing that leaves behind a graphic emptiness. Acinematography, writing as removal, removing, removement. **Invisibility.** The invisibility that permeates Deanimated is marked by a disorder: many characters seem to see what has been erased. Not a genuine invisibility, but a visibility marked by the absence of bodies. The house acts as the center of the film, the human characters afterthoughts, accidents, useless movements that periodically traverse the profilmic space. Deanimated circumvents the body, circumscribes and circumcises it: here, as in Arnold's earlier works, the body is itself an excess: unsightly, excremental. In Deanimated, visuality does not originate in, nor does it return to the body. Human bodies are slight interferences in the trajectory of an empty visuality, an inhuman visuality of the camera.

Another form of invisibility plays throughout Deanimated in the figure of the black butler, Evans. (See **Evans**, below.) **Interval.** Arnold's work has inserted throughout the film intervals that reroute the logical flow of the original. Those intervals are often sites of massive immobility, points of unbearable frustration at the inaction of the body. Arnold's bodies are always under only a partial erasure: something is left. A mild convulsion, irrepressible twitches, looks into and from nowhere, sometimes an effect that lingers in the place of an erasure. A trace of the erasure as an ex-sign, an intensity. (The fantasy of a sign of intensity, a graphics of the unimaginable.) **Incest.** The triangle of father, absent mother, daughter is enhanced in Arnold's revision of the original. Like the exaggerations that charge the obscene familial gestures of Alone - Andy Hardy rubbing his mother's shoulders and thrusting his body into her from behind while she licks her lips and flutters her eyes - the imposed restraint between father and daughter, the slight brushes between them, and a few lapses and changed lines in Deanimated produce an electric, Electra-l, anti-Oedipus. Oedipus, who had his feet pierced at infancy, and whose name bears the sign of his crippling - "swollen feet" - is, like Kessler, always in the wrong place at the wrong time, a master criminal-victim.

Es ist keine wirkliche Unsichtbarkeit, sondern eine Sichtbarkeit, die durch die Abwesenheit von Körpern geprägt ist. Das Haus bildet das Zentrum des Films als wäre es geschaffen für die nachträglichen Einfälle der Figuren, ihre Missgeschicke und nutzlosen Bewegungen, die mit gewisser Regelmäßigkeit den Raum vor der Kamera durchqueren. *Deanimated* umgeht den Körper, umschreibt und umkreist ihn: hier - wie auch schon in Arnolds früheren Arbeiten - ist der Körper selbst ein Exzess: unansehnlich, exkremental. In *Deanimated* beginnt die Sichtbarkeit nicht mit dem Körper und sie kehrt auch nicht zu ihm zurück. Menschliche Körper sind lediglich geringfügige Widerstände in der Bahn einer leeren Visualität, des *unmenschlichen* Blicks der Kamera.

Eine weitere Form der Unsichtbarkeit manifestiert sich in *Deanimated* in der Gestalt des schwarzen Butlers, Evans. (Siehe **Evans**, weiter unten.) **Intervall**. Arnold hat in seiner Bearbeitung dem Film Intervalle eingeschrieben, die den logischen Fluss des Originals um-leiten. Diese Intervalle sind häufig Orte massiver Unbeweglichkeit, Stätten einer unerträglichen Frustration über die Untätigkeit des Körpers. Arnolds Körper stehen immer unter dem Verdikt einer teilweisen Auslöschung: „etwas" bleibt zurück. Eine leichte Verkrampfung, ein unbeherrschtes Zucken, Blicke in das oder aus dem Nichts, manchmal ein Effekt, der den Ort einer Auslöschung markiert. Eine Spur des Ausgelöschten als Ex-Zeichen, als Intensität. (Das Phantasma eines Zeichens für Intensität, einer Grafik des Unvorstellbaren.) **Inzest**. Das Dreieck aus Vater, abwesender Mutter und Tochter erhält in Arnolds Bearbeitung verstärkte Präsenz. Ähnlich den obszönen familiären Gesten in *Alone* - Andy Hardy, der die Schultern seiner Mutter massiert und sich mit seinem Körper von hinten an sie herandrückt, während sie sich die Lippen leckt und mit den Augen rollt-, produzieren die erzwungene Zurückhaltung zwischen Vater und Tochter, das leichte Aneinanderstreifen der beiden, der eine oder andere Lapsus und ein paar vertauschte Textzeilen in *Deanimated* einen elektrischen, *Elektra*-len, Anti-Ödipus. Ödipus, dem als Kind die Knöchel seiner Füße durchbohrt wurden, und dessen Name das Zeichen dieser Verletzung trägt - „Schwellfuß" -, ist so wie Kessler stets zur falschen Zeit am falschen Ort, die meisterliche Kombination von Täter und Opfer. (Wie Ödipus verschließt sich auch Kessler der Erkenntnis, dass er selbst jene Verbrechen begeht, die ihn so sehr beunruhigen.) Arnold beschreibt eine seiner Annäherungen an die „symptomatische Schauspielkunst", die er in *Deanimated* unternommen hat, folgendermaßen:

„Zum einen geht es um das „Herumhängen", die Schauspieler sehen so aus, als ob sie sich ausruhen würden oder träumend auf ihren Auftritt warten. Aber sie sind entweder zu früh oder zu spät dran. Das ist interessant, weil es den üblichen Erwartungen widerspricht. Schauspieler „spielen" normalerweise in Filmen, sie

(Like Oedipus, Kessler fails to realize he is the perpetrator of the crimes that disturb him so much.) Arnold describes one of his approaches to the symptomatic acting he has engendered in *Deanimated*:

"One is the "hanging around" approach, they look as if they are relaxing, dreaming, waiting for the part they can act out, but they're either too early or too late. I think that's interesting, because it contradicts the usual expectations: actors are usually acting in feature films, they usually have something to do or to say, they don't hang around - hanging around in front of the camera is a Warhol-like approach that didn't exist in the 40s. Back then (times were better) actors were still actors and they had to act. That's what they were paid for. In *Deanimated* we're looking at actors in their spare time, Warholian actors that were born too early." [13]

Adirecting, "*la mise hors scène*," says Lyotard. [14] A cast of Oedipuses limping behind the crime and its investigation, always arriving too late, only to discover they have already been there. **Investigation.** *The Invisible Ghost* and *Deanimated* operate according to the narrative structure of detection and investigation, the resolution of a string of murders. While *The Invisible Ghost* moves, however lamely, toward closure, *Deanimated* reveals less and less, until blackness overtakes the final minutes of Arnold's revision. An inverted Oedipal structure in the form of an absented mother, a father and daughter left together, an epidemic of blindness, or invisibility, which over-takes the house, ultimately the work. The film has been blinded, has succumbed to the Oedipalizing force of erasure, every spectator blinded and silenced, like Oedipus in the end. When the **Inspector**, whose task consists of vigilance, investigation (inspection), and **interrogation**, succumbs to the mute and inarticulate order of Arnold's house, the edifice of audio-visuality itself seems to have collapsed.

Arnold's *Deanimated* is accompanied by two companion works, shorter, erased and morphed loops from *All About Eve* (Joseph L. Mankiewicz, 1950) and *High Noon* (Fred Zinneman, 1952). The three erasures, which form a triptych, are in fact **installations**. By moving the screening space from a theater (where Arnold's earlier works were projected) to a specific installation site, consisting of three works projected across five screens, Arnold has marked the break from cinema to ambient space, televisuality, digital video. But the break is not primarily technological in nature, but across the temperature of visual media - the cool spaces that Arnold occupies allow one to sense the de-animation of film, the cooling of cinema into the folds of other media. The emphasis is never technological in Arnold's media - although the techniques are dazzling - but rather symptomatic. Technological functions illuminate the excesses and deficits of the image. A superficial **interiority** opens within each work, but also as a set of installations; the line that

haben etwas zu tun oder zu sagen, sie hängen nicht herum - vor der Kamera herumzuhängen, ist eine Erfindung von Warhol, die in den 40er Jahren noch nicht existierte. Damals, die Zeiten waren noch besser, waren die Schauspieler noch Schauspieler und sie mussten schauspielen. Dafür wurden sie schließlich auch bezahlt. In *Deanimated* sehen wir Schauspieler in ihrer Freizeit, Warhol'-sche Schauspieler, die einfach zu früh geboren worden sind."[13]

Die Exszenierung, „*la mise hors scène*", sagt Lyotard.[14] Ein Ensemble von Ödipussen, die dem Verbrechen und seiner Aufklärung hinterher humpeln, die immer zu spät kommen, nur um festzustellen, dass sie bereits einmal da gewesen sind. **Ermittlung**. *The Invisible Ghost* und *Deanimated* funktionieren gemäß der Erzählstruktur von Detektivarbeit und Ermittlung, der Aufklärung einer Serie von Morden. Während *The Invisible Ghost*, wie lahm auch immer, einer Lösung zustrebt, enthüllt *Deanimated* zusehends weniger, bis sich schließlich Dunkelheit über die letzten Minuten der Arnoldschen Bearbeitung legt. Die umgekehrte ödipale Struktur in Form einer abwesenden Mutter, eines Vater und einer Tochter, die gemeinsam zurückbleiben, eine Epidemie der Blindheit oder der Unsichtbarkeit, die das Haus und letztendlich auch das Werk selbst einholt. Der Film wurde gleichsam geblendet, er unterwirft sich erblindet der ödipalisierenden Gewalt der Auslöschung, und auch den Betrachter ereilt – wie Ödipus am Ende – dieses Schicksal. Wenn der **Inspektor**, dessen Aufgabe darin besteht, Wachsamkeit zu üben, Einblicke zu gewinnen (zu inspizieren) und **Verhöre** zu führen, sich der stummen und sprachlosen Ordnung des Arnoldschen Hauses ergibt, scheint das Gebäude der Audio-Visualität selbst einzustürzen.

Arnolds *Deanimated* wird von zwei weiteren Arbeiten begleitet: kürzeren, teilweise ausgelöschten und gemorphten Loops aus *All About Eve* (Joseph L. Mankiewicz, 1950) und aus *High Noon* (Fred Zinneman, 1952). Die drei Auslöschungen, die insgesamt ein Triptychon bilden, sind in der Tat **Installationen**. Mit dem Wechsel des Vorführorts von einem Lichtspieltheater (wo Arnolds frühere Arbeiten gezeigt wurden) zu einem spezifischen Installationsort, an dem die drei Arbeiten auf fünf Leinwänden projiziert werden, hat Arnold auch den Bruch vom Kino zur ambienten Räumlichkeit, zur Televisualität, zum digitalen Video vollzogen. Aber der Bruch ist kein primär technologischer, sondern führt quer über das Temperaturspektrum der visuellen Medien - die kalten Orte, die Arnold besetzt, lassen die De-Animation des Films erspüren, das Abkühlen des Kinos im Verbund der neuen Medien. Die Betonung erschöpft sich bei Arnold jedoch nie im Technologischen - trotz atemberaubender Techniken -, sondern zielt auf das Symptomatische. Technische Funktionen machen die Exzesse und Defizite der Bilder sichtbar. Eine an der Oberfläche situierte **Innenansicht** öffnet sich innerhalb jeder einzel-

separates life from animation, image from experience, excess from deficit no longer falls on the screen, but seeps into the architecture.

Nihilism. The nihilism that Lyotard rejects is different from the asystemic eliminations of Arnold's work. The **nothings** that linger in *Deanimated* form a material presence, a form of haunting. The very term elimination is a solecism, since only the figures are eliminated from the surface of the narrative: what is not seen is the substitution of a trace, the material inscription of something else that replaces the missing figure in the form of nothing. There, invisible, but perceptible. Looking at nothing, watching someone looking at nothing, following empty points-of-view is not a nihilism as such. There is, in *Deanimated*, extensive annihilation, the destruction of "the unity of an organic body." This is not a nihilism (a politics of total destruction), but a reversal of the nihilistic tendency of the commercial cinema, a rejection of the despair that envelopes the very desire for order. Following the spirit of Lyotard's language, one could say, an *anihilism*.

Erasure. For Lyotard, the economy of cinema operates on the principles of "exclusions and effacements." [15] In his schema, exclusions are largely unconscious, effacements are part of the active work of eliminating useless movements. But Arnold's gestures are neither, since they are both conscious and unconscious erasures, and circulate within an entirely distinct film economy from that articulated by Lyotard. The **exclusions** that spread throughout *Deanimated* are material forms of emptiness, excretions on the surface of the film, stains rather than negations. **Effacement** is an even more complex issue in Arnold's work, because the rearranged faces of *Deanimated* are not effacements in the ordinary sense of the term. The morphographic closures, especially of mouths, can be considered the exact contrary of effacement, materially and conceptually. Surfacing or resurfacing rather than effacing. The butler **Evans**, for example, represents a key resurface in Arnold's recycled work. In the reworked version he is, Arnold notes, "the only character regularly referred to by name," and serves as a key conduit between the various rooms and moments of the narrative. From a ubiquitous and invisible device in the original, Arnold has turned Evans into a central figure of the perverted narrative. Already only **extra**, Evans's visibility has been enhanced in *Deanimated*, perhaps the only character to increase in this register. By disfiguring the actors, Arnold has reconfigured Evans, moving him from an already effaced extra, to a central figure in the new economy of paralyzed life. He has been ***erased*** from the film, which is to say, his race has become visible.

In one scene, Evans rushes into Kessler's room early in the morning after discovering the murdered body of the maid (which Arnold has erased). Leaning onto the sleeping Kessler's bed, Evans whispers, "Mr. Kessler," ("Yes?") "something terrible has hap-

nen Arbeit, aber vor allem auch in der Serie der Installationen; die Linie, die das Leben vom Belebtsein, das Bild von der Erfahrung und den Überschuss vom Mangel trennt, fällt hier nicht mehr auf die Leinwand, sondern sickert in die Architektur hinein.

Nihilismus. Der Nihilismus, den Lyotard zurückweist, unterscheidet sich von den asystemischen Eliminierungen in Arnolds Werk. Denn das **Nichts**, das in *Deanimated* andauert, bildet eine materielle Präsenz, eine Art von Spuk. Der Ausdruck „Ausschluss" selbst wäre hier ein sprachlicher Missgriff, da einzig die Figuren von der Oberfläche der Erzählung entfernt wurden: was nicht gesehen wird, ist die Substitution einer Spur, die materielle Einschreibung von etwas anderem, das die fehlende Personen in der Form des Nichts ersetzt. Sie ist da, zwar unsichtbar, aber dennoch wahrnehmbar. Das Nichts anzusehen, jemanden zu beobachten, der das Nichts ansieht, leeren Blickachsen zu folgen, ist an sich kein Nihilismus. *Deanimated* zeigt die ausgiebige Vernichtung, die Zerstörung „der Einheit eines organischen Körpers". Das ist kein Nihilismus (eine Politik der totalen Zerstörung), sondern eine Umkehrung der nihilistischen Tendenz des Kommerzkinos, ein Zurückweisen der Verzweiflung, die das Begehren nach Ordnung umfasst. Lyotards Gedanken folgend, könnte man hier von einem *Anihilismus* sprechen.

Auslöschungen. Für Lyotard funktioniert die Ökonomie des Kinos nach den Prinzipien des „Ausschließens und Auslöschens".[15] Seinem Modell nach erfolgen Ausschlüsse größtteils unbewusst, während Auslöschungen Teil der aktiven Arbeit des Eliminierens unbrauchbarer Bewegungen sind. Aber Arnolds Gesten sind weder das eine noch das andere, da sie sowohl bewusste wie unbewusste Auslöschungen sind und innerhalb einer vollkommen anderen Filmökonomie zirkulieren als jener, die Lyotard beschrieben hat. Die **Ausschlüsse**, die sich in *Deanimated* ausbreiten, sind materielle Formen der Leere, **Ausscheidungen** an der Oberfläche des Films, eher Verunreinigungen als Verneinungen. Die **Auslöschung** ist ein noch komplexeres Thema in Arnolds Filminstallation, weil die neu arrangierten Gesichter in *Deanimated* nicht auf Auslöschungen im üblichen Wortsinn beruhen. Die morphographisch erzeugten Verschlüsse, insbesondere der Münder, sind das Gegenteil einer Auslöschung, sowohl materiell wie konzeptionell. Ein Auftauchen und Wiedererscheinen statt eines Ausgelöscht-Werdens. Der Butler, **Evans** beispielsweise stellt eine zentrale Figur des Wiederauftauchens in Arnolds recycliertem Werk dar. In der bearbeiteten Version ist er, wie Arnold anmerkt, „die einzige Figur, die regelmäßig mit Namen genannt wird", er dient als ein wichtiges Verbindungsglied zwischen den verschiedenen Räumen und Bedeutungsmomenten der Erzählung. Von einem zwar allgegenwärtigen, doch unsichtbaren Diener im Original hat Arnold nun Evans zu einer Zentralfigur seiner

pened." What follows are series of exchanges, silent intensities, where Arnold has suppressed the ensuing dialogue and sealed their mouths. The encounter concludes when Kessler says, "Call the police, I'll see what I can do." The exchange between Kessler and Evans, over-determined by the aesthetic, political, social, racial, and gendered functions of the human figure in 1941, has been **expropriated**, emptied, and reduced to a comical and touching series of inarticulate exchanges between an interracial couple in and over a bed. Evans has assumed the figure of a nervous intruder, a tentative predator (a stereotype buried in the figure of the black domestic). What has happened in the span of the morph, a partial seduction? An **expressive** communication of desire? What has been eliminated is the infrastructure that determines and over-determines the encounter, leaving behind only the **erotic** vacuum of pure, disfigured intensities.

Martin Arnold. The Japanese concept *ma*, space, refers to the interstices that constitute aesthetic space and experience, perhaps what Vertov meant by "interval." It appears, in Lyotard's notion of the renunciation of bodily totality in art and theater, when he invokes the "almost imperceptible movements of the Nô theater."[16] The romantic **ma**teriality of Lyotard's acinema has been transfigured - muted, mutated, mutilated - in *Deanimated* into prevocal murmurs and mutterings. (Mutter, mother.) **Ma**ternity, a feminized cinema - "la cinema," "ma cinema" - erupts in *Deanimated* in the figure of a negated and absent mother. (Murderer.) The missing mother, the phantom mother who haunts and destroys the house and its occupants, produces all around her a "**mad**house architecture," according to Arnold, in which the human figures seem intellectually and emotionally crippled, drugged, or hypnotized. **Ma**lcontent, **ma**lfunctioning. Like the homicidal mother already inside Kessler (a **ma**le mother, M**A**LE, and prototype Nor**ma**n Bates), *Deanimated* renders maternity within **mas**culinity, a parasite maternity, "ma" and "pa" cinema - a polymorphology of cinema, gender, and the sexes.

One effect of Lyotard's neologism is that it establishes a kind of cyclical word, a faux palindrome that invokes Duch**a**mp's anagram, "anemic." Words that fold into and disappear into other words. Arnold's revision infects the inhabitants of Kessler's house with a form of anemia, the gradual loss of red blood cells, oxygen, and energy in a decreasing, inverse animation, de-animation. Movement and paralysis, vitality and exhaustion, image and erasure, cinema and anemia set the limits of *Deanimated*. Movement, repetition, repeal, removal. "The acinema," says Lyotard, "would be situated at the two poles of … extreme immobilization and extreme mobilization."

"It is only in *thought* that these two modes are incompatible. In a libidinal economy they are, on the contrary, necessarily asso-

pervertierten Geschichte erhoben. Evans, der im Original bloß ein **Nebendarsteller** war, gewinnt in *Deanimated* an Sichtbarkeit und Bedeutung, vielleicht die einzige Figur, der im neuen Zeichenregime Wachstum zugebilligt wird. Indem er die Schauspieler entstellt, hat Arnold die Gestalt des Evans neu konfiguriert und ihn von einem ursprünglich kaum wahrnehmbaren Statisten zu einer zentralen Figur in der neuen Ökonomie des paralysierten Lebens gemacht. Er wurde aus dem Film *‚eraced'*, das heißt, seine Rasse ist nun sichtbar geworden.

In einer Szene eilt Evans frühmorgens in Kesslers Zimmer, nachdem er die Leiche des Zimmermädchens (von Arnold ausgelöscht) entdeckt hat. Sich über das Bett mit dem schlafenden Kessler beugend, flüstert Evans: „Mr. Kessler", ("Ja?"), „etwas Schreckliches ist geschehen." Was dann folgt, ist eine Serie von Blickkontakten, stillen Intensitäten, in denen Arnold den ursprünglichen Dialog unterdrückt und die Münder der Protagonisten versiegelt. Die Begegnung endet, als Kessler sagt: „Rufen Sie die Polizei, ich werde sehen, was ich tun kann." Der Austausch zwischen Kessler und Evans, überdeterminiert von den ästhetischen, politischen, gesellschaftlichen, ethnischen und geschlechtsspezifischen Funktionen des Menschenbildes des Jahres 1941, ist **enteignet**, ausgeleert und reduziert worden auf eine Reihe komischer und zugleich rührender Gesten eines stummen Verkehrs zwischen einem gemischtrassigen Paar in und über einem Bett. Evans hat die Gestalt eines nervösen Eindringlings angenommen, eines versuchten Räubers (eine stereotype Vorstellung, die der Gestalt des schwarzen Hausangestellten zugrunde liegt). Was ist in der Zeitspanne dieses Morphs geschehen? Eine partielle Verführung? Die **expressive** Mitteilung eines Begehrens? Was eliminiert worden ist, ist die Infrastruktur, die die Begegnung determiniert und überdeterminiert hat, womit einzig das **erotische** Vakuum von reinen, disfigurierten Intensitäten zurückbleibt.

Martin Arnold. Das japanische Konzept des *ma* für Raum bezieht sich auf jenen Zwischenraum, der sich zwischen dem ästhetischen Raum und der Erfahrung auftut, vielleicht das, was Vertov mit „Intervall" meinte. Dieses erscheint in Lyotards Vorstellung vom Verzicht auf die körperliche Totalität in der Kunst und im Theater dort, wo er die „kaum wahrnehmbaren Bewegungen des Nô-Theaters"[16] erwähnt. Die romantische **Materialität** von Lyotards *Acinéma* wurde in *Deanimated* verändert - zum Schweigen gebracht, mutiert, verstümmelt - hin zu einem prävokalem Gemurmel und Geraune. (Mutter, mother.) Die **Maternität**, ein feminisiertes Kino - „la cinéma", „ma cinéma" - birst in *Deanimated* in Gestalt einer verneinten und abwesenden Mutter hervor. (Mörderin.) Die fehlende Mutter, die Phantom-Mutter, die das Haus und seine Bewohner heimsucht und zerstört, produziert eine Narrenhaus-Architektur (**Ma**dhouse), in der, wie Arnold betont,

ciated; stupefaction, terror, anger, hate, pleasure - all the intensities - are always displacements in place. We should read the term emotion as a motion moving toward its own exhaustion, an immobilizing motion, an immobilized mobilization."[17]
Acinema. A word that begins and ends in "a" and engendering reversibility, like Arnold's earlier film, *Alone*. At the end of cinema, in the mark of its negation, is its beginning in the circular "a" that recycles cinema, acinema. Of the premature blackout that consumes the final minutes of *Deanimated*, (**M**) Arnold notes, "no light, no cinema, not even an acinema."[18] Only the "a" remains and returns, the negation of cinema, its beginning and end, recycled again and again, **Arnold**.

die menschlichen Gestalten intellektuell und emotional verkrüppelt wirken, wie unter Drogen gesetzt oder hypnotisiert. Unzu-
frieden, funktionsunfähig. (**Ma**lcontent, **mal**functioning.) So wie
die mörderische Mutter, die bereits von Kessler innerlich Besitz
ergriffen hat (eine männliche Mutter, **MA**LE, ein Prototypus von
Nor**ma**n Bates), stellt *Deanimated* die Mutterschaft in der
Maennlichkeit dar, eine parasitäre Mütterlichkeit: „Ma"- und „Pa"-
Kino - eine Polymorphologie des Kinos, der Geschlechterrollen
und der Geschlechter selbst.

Ein Effekt von Lyotards Neologismus, *Acinéma*, ist die Etablierung einer Art zyklischen Wortes, eines „verunglückten Pa-
lindroms", das an Duch**am**ps Anagramm „anemic" erinnert. Wörter kreuzen einander und verschwinden in anderen Wörtern.
Arnolds Bearbeitung infiziert die Bewohner von Kesslers Haus
mit einer Form von Anämie, dem allmählichen Verlust von roten
Blutkörperchen, von Sauerstoff und Energie, in einer abneh-
menden, inversen Animation, einer De-Animation. Bewegung
und Paralyse, Vitalität und Erschöpfung, Bild und Auslöschung,
Cinéma und Anämie bestimmen die Grenzen von *Deanimated*.
Bewegung, Wiederholung, Aufhebung, Beseitigung. „L'Acinéma
befände sich", sagt Lyotard, „an den beiden Polen ... der äußersten
Immobilisierung und der äußersten Mobilisierung."

„Nur für das *Denken* sind diese beiden Modi unvereinbar. In
der Libidoökonomie sind sie dagegen notwendig verbunden; die
Verblüffung, der Schrecken, der Zorn, der Hass, die Lust - alle Intensitäten - sind immer Verschiebungen an Ort und Stelle. Man
sollte das Wort *Erregung* (Emotion) wohl als eine bis zur Selbst-
erschöpfung gehende *Regung* analysieren, als Immobilisie-
rungsbewegung, als immobilisierte Mobilisierung."[17]

Acinéma. Ein Wort, das mit dem Buchstaben „a" anfängt und
aufhört und Umkehrbarkeit erzeugt, so wie Arnolds früherer Film
Alone. Am Ende des Kinos, im Zeichen seiner Verneinung, liegt
sein Ursprung in jenem kreisförmigen „a", das Cinéma und Acinéma recycelt. Zum vorzeitigen Black-Out, das die finalen Minuten
von *Deanimated* verschlingt, merkt (**M**) Arnold an: „Kein Licht,
kein Kino, nicht einmal ein Acinéma."[18] Nur das „a" bleibt übrig
und kehrt zurück, die Verneinung des Cinéma, sein Anfang und
Ende, wieder und immer wieder recycelt, **Arnold**.

| 1 Jean-François Lyotard, „L'Acinéma", in: Cinéma: Théorie, lectures (Paris: Ed.
Klincksieck, 1973). English translation, Jean-François Lyotard, „Acinema", in:
Narrative, Apparatus, Ideology: A Film Theory Reader, ed. Philip Rosen, trans.
Paisley N. Livingston (New York: Columbia University Press, 1986), p 349-59.
| 2 Lyotard, „Acinema", p 349. | 3 Lyotard, „Acinema", p 349. | 4 Lyotard, „Acinema",
p 349. | 5 Lyotard, „Acinema", p 350. | 6 Lyotard, „Acinema", p 355. | 7 Lyotard,
„Acinema", p 350. | 8 Lyotard, „Acinema", p 355. Le film est le corps organique des
mouvements cinématographiques. " | 9 Lyotard, „Acinema", p 351. | 10 Arnold
describes morphing, a form of digital compositing, as „a combination of the
techniques of warping and dissolving between two images over a specific period
of time. Dissolving is known from classical cinema. Warping is a method of
distorting an image. Conceptually, it is easiest to think of warping as if your image
were printed on a thin sheet of flexible rubber. This rubber sheet can be pushed
and pulled by various amounts in various areas until the desired result is obtained."
Conversation with Martin Arnold, 12 August 2002. | 11 Lyotard, „Acinema", p 355
(original emphases). | 12 Conversation with Martin Arnold, 16 July 2002. | 13
Conversation with Martin Arnold, 3 August 2002. The second approach is the
„confused intellectually / emotionally crippled" approach, which throughout
Deanimated creates a sense of irreducible disorientation. The third approach,
which Arnold has strived to minimize, is what he calls the "Invisible Man" approach,
a kind of 1950s special effects look. | 14 Lyotard, „Acinema", p 354. | 15 Lyotard,
„Acinema", p 353. | 16 Lyotard, „Acinema", p 358. | 17 Lyotard, „Acinema", p 356
(original emphases). | 18 Conversation with Martin Arnold, 8 August 2002.

| 1 Jean-Francois Lyotard, „L'Acinéma", in: [Kino: Theorie, Vorlesungen] (Paris: Ed.
Klincksieck, 1973). [Englische Übersetzung, Jean-Francois Lyotard, „Acinema", in:
Erzählung, Apparat, Ideologie: Ein Filmtheorie-Reader, Hg. von Philip Rosen, Übers. v.
Paisley N. Livingston] (New York: Columbia University Press, 1986), S. 349-59. | 2
Lyotard, „Acinema", S. 349. | 3 Lyotard, „Acinema", S. 349. | 4 Lyotard, „Acinema", S.
349. | 5 Lyotard, „Acinema", S. 350. | 6 Lyotard, „Acinema", S. 355. | 7 Lyotard, „Acinema",
S. 350. | 8 Lyotard, „Acinema", S. 355. „Le film est le corps organique des mouvements
cinématographiques." [Der Film ist der organische Körper der kinematographischen
Bewegungen.] | 9 Lyotard, „Acinema", S. 351. | 10 Arnold beschreibt das Morphen, eine
Form des Digital Compositing, als „eine Kombination der Technik des Warping bei
gleichzeitiger Überblendung zwischen zwei Bildern innerhalb einer bestimmten
Zeitspanne. Blenden kennt man aus dem klassischen Kino. Warping ist eine Methode
der Verzerrung eines Bildes. Im Prinzip kann man sich dabei ein Bild vorstellen, das auf
eine dünne Schicht beweglichen Gummis aufgetragen ist. Diese Gummihaut kann in
verschiedene Richtungen gezogen werden, solange bis das gewünschte Ergebnis erzielt
wird." Gespräch mit Martin Arnold, 12. August 2002. | 11 Lyotard, „Acinema", S. 355
(Kursiv im Original). | 12 Gespräch mit Martin Arnold, 16. Juli 2002. | 13 Gespräch mit
Martin Arnold, 3. August 2002. Die zweite Herangehensweise ist die „intellektuell
verwirrte bzw emotional verkrüppelte", die im gesamten Verlauf von Deanimated ein
Gefühl der Orientierungslosigkeit hervorruft. Die dritte Strategie, und Arnold war
bemüht, sie auf ein Minimum zu reduzieren, ist die des „Invisible Man"-Look. Arnold
meint damit die billigen Special Effects der Science Fiction Filme der 50er Jahre, wo
unsichtbare Gestalten Türen öffnen und diverse Gegenstände bewegen.
| 14 Lyotard, „Acinema", S. 354. | 15 Lyotard, „Acinema", S. 353. | 16 Lyotard, „Acinema",
S. 358. | 17 Lyotard, „Acinema", S. 356 (Kursiv im Original). | 18 Gespräch mit Martin
Arnold, 8. August 2002.

*

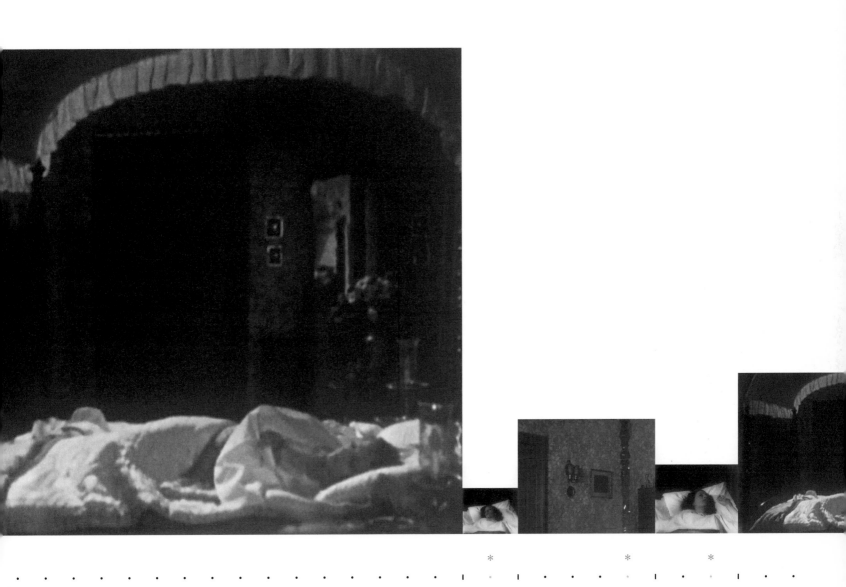

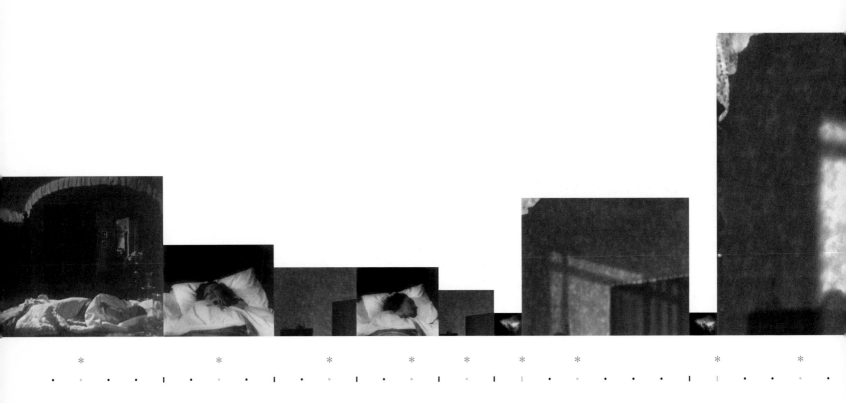

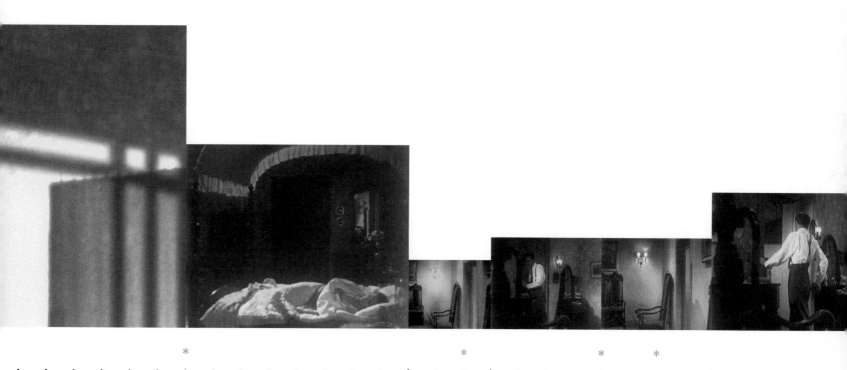

*

*   *   *

Are you all right, Evans?

No, sir.

Is something wrong?

You have no idea how happy I am to see you.

Come out! Come on out, I say.

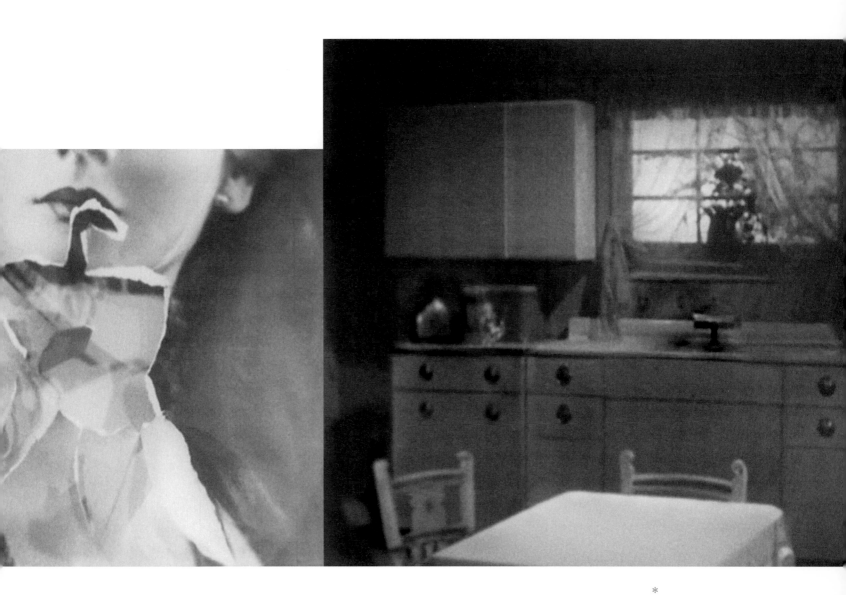

*

. . . . | . . . .

43

*
. . . .

*

Vom Dasein des Verschwundenen

Wolfgang Pircher

Medien haben ihren Spaß an Paradoxien, das ist eine ihrer liebenswerten Eigenschaften. Nachdem beispielsweise in Thomas Bernhards *Auslöschung* die Erzählfigur ihre pathologische Familien- und Landesgeschichte abgearbeitet hat, eine Arbeit, die von der physischen Auslöschung eines Teils ihrer Familie ausgelöst wurde, beabsichtigt sie ihrerseits den Heimatort Wolfsegg „auszulöschen". Dieses soll geschehen, indem die Verworfenheit und Gemeinheit seiner Bewohner abkonterfeit wird. „Wir tragen alle ein Wolfsegg mit uns herum und haben den Willen, es auszulöschen zu unserer Errettung, es, indem wir es aufschreiben wollen, vernichten wollen, auslöschen."[1]

Nun, das Medium Buch speichert ungerührt diese „Auslöschung", lässt Wolfsegg also in jedem Leser wieder aufleben und somit keineswegs verschwinden. Es wird geradezu als „ausgelöscht", nämlich im moralischen Sinne, erhalten, und zwar solange das Medium dauert. Medien aber leben auch nicht ewig. Auch und schon gar nicht in jener Form, die zwar durch und durch verlogen, so Bernhard, „aber für den Großteil der Menschheit, die gewünschte und die ideale ist"[2], nämlich die Photographie.

Film und Photographie sind Medien des Verschwindens, der Auslöschung. Nicht nur nimmt das Trägermaterial bei zu langen Belichtungszeiten sich bewegende Objekte nicht auf, sondern das Material selbst lässt sich in seiner chemischen Reaktion nur verlangsamen, aber der Selbstauslöschungsprozess nicht für immer verhindern. Damit sind Film und Photographie Speichermedien, deren technischen Formen insgesamt ein physisches Vergessen, eine notwendige Löschung des auf sie nur vorläufig Gebannten eigen ist. Aber Medien sind verschaltbar, so dass, was in der einen Form zu verlöschen droht, in einer anderen wieder erhalten werden kann und so fort bis ans Ende aller Medientage. Was aber ist es, das so über die Medien hinweggleitet, um da und dort halt zu machen, diesen oder jenen Träger zu benutzen? Wir jedenfalls wissen, ohne diesen Träger ist dieses Etwas schlicht ein Nichts für uns, ohne ihn existiert es für uns nicht. Natürlich wird man einwenden, dass dieses Etwas aber doch nicht dem Träger entspringt, sondern ihm sich gleichsam von wo anders her assoziiert. Flüchtig wie es ist, verdankt es bloß sein diesseitiges Leben der zeitweiligen Beharrlichkeit des Trägers, der es zur Erscheinung bringt, was heißt der privaten Vorstellung entreißt und es prinzipiell in den öffentlichen Raum stellt.

Jede technologische Transformation verändert zugleich die Bedingungen der technischen Intervention, somit stellt sie nicht einfach eine Verdopplung des Gegebenen dar, sondern eine Versetzung in einen anderen Raum der Bearbeitbarkeit. Wir können das in der Transformation von analogem Film in digitale Aufzeichnung mitverfolgen. Was in der einen Form den Beschränkungen des Photos unterworfen ist, nämlich nur speichern

On the Presence of the Vanished

Wolfgang Pircher

The media like to have their fun with paradoxes, this is one of their lovable qualities. For example, in Thomas Bernhard's *Extinction,* the narrator-character, having worked through his pathological family and local history, a labour triggered off by the physical extinction of part of his family, decides, in turn, to "wipe out" his home-town of Wolfsegg. This is to be achieved by a portrayal of the depravity and baseness of its inhabitants. "We all carry a Wolfsegg inside us and intend to eliminate it for our own salvation, wishing, by writing it up, to destroy it, to extinguish it."[1]

Well, the medium of the book quite imperturbably stores this "extinction", allowing Wolfsegg to get a new lease on life within each reader, and thus not to disappear at all. It is, in a way, retrieved as "extinguished", specifically in the moral sense, and will in fact be retained for as long as the medium itself may last. Yet, media do not live forever, either. This is especially true of the medium which, according to Bernhard, may be mendacious through and through, "yet which, for the major part of humanity, is the desirable and ideal one"[2], to wit, photography.

Cinematography and photography are media of disappearance, of dissolution. Not only does the carrier material, upon protracted exposure to light, fail to record moving objects, the material itself undergoes a chemical process leading to its eventual disintegration, which can only be slowed down but never permanently halted. Film and photography are thus storage media, whose technical forms are, all told, heir to a physical oblivion, a necessary extinction of all that has been only temporarily captured upon them. But media are interchangeable, so that, what is threatened to be lost in the one shape may be preserved in another, and so continue on till the end of all media days. Still the question remains: what actually is this thing that glides over all the media, halting for a comfort stop here and there, using one carrier or another? We know that without the carrier this something would be simply a nothing to us, that without the one the other would not exist. Of course, it can be objected that this something does not emanate from the carrier itself but links up to it, as it were, by an association from outside. Fleeting, as it is, this substance owes its earthly existence only to the temporary persistence of the carrier, which bears forth its appearance, extricating it from a private concept and placing it squarely in the public space.

Every technological transformation simultaneously alters the conditions of technical intervention. It does not, therefore, present simply a duplication of the given, but a transposition into another space of processability. We can observe this in the transformation of analogue film to digital recording. What is subject to the limitations of the photograph in the one shape, that is, of only being able to store what can be placed literally before the camera eye under certain, defined conditions (of size, light, and speed), and

zu können, was unter bestimmten definierten Bedingungen (Größe, Licht, Geschwindigkeit) buchstäblich vor die Kamera gestellt werden kann, und sei es auch nur als potemkinsche Kulisse, das ist in der anderen Form gleichsam aus dem Inneren der Apparatur schöpfbar. Insofern im digitalen Medium jeder Bildpunkt konstruierbar ist, stellt das Erscheinen-lassen des nahezu Beliebigen nicht mehr jene alte Schwerfälligkeit des analogen Mediums dar, alles irgendwie zu bauen und vor die Kamera schleppen zu müssen.

Aber der Prozess, welcher etwas zur Darstellung bringen kann, lässt sich auch umkehren. Natürlich entdeckt es sich bald, dass der Film nur angehalten werden muss, um etwas aus ihm entfernen zu können, das beim neuerlichen Start als *verschwunden* erscheint. Im Unterschied zum realen Geschehen lässt sich der Filmstreifen *schneiden*. Aber immer noch befinden wir uns im gleichsam physischen Raum eines körperlichen Mediums, das den eigentlichen Prozess nur von außen erfassen kann. Der Wechsel ins Medium der inneren Bearbeitbarkeit, wie sie die elektronische Bilderzeugung ermöglicht, verändert naturgemäß die Beziehung zum Bild selbst, genauer zum Bildinhalt. Das elektronische Werkzeug greift die Erzählung selbst an.

Der von Martin Arnold bearbeitete Film *The Invisible Ghost* zeigt, getreu seinem Titel, vielfältige Formen des Verschwindens und der Rückkehr. Da ist einmal die verschwundene Gattin, deren Porträt im Vorraum des Hauses hängt und später zerschnitten wird. Immer wieder kehrt sie aus ihrer Verborgenheit zurück, um damit allerdings eine andere Art des Verschwindens auszulösen: die Trance, also das Verschwinden des klaren Bewusstseins ihres Gatten, der, sobald er sie am Fenster erblickt, vom Abgrund seines Wahnes verschlungen wird und daran geht, junge Mädchen oder den Gärtner verschwinden zu machen, d. h. auszulöschen, umzubringen. Nach der Tat aber kehrt er wieder in seinen Geist zurück, in sein Bewusstsein, um mit Bedauern zur Kenntnis zu nehmen, dass die von ihm begangene Tat, die er nicht als die seine *weiß*, nunmehr den Freund seiner Tochter zum Verschwinden bringt. Dieser wird als der Tat verdächtig schuldig gesprochen und flugs hingerichtet, um alsbald in der Gestalt des täuschend ähnlichen Bruders wiederaufzutauchen.

Man könnte weitere solcher Serien entdecken und meinen, dieser Film sei eine ziemlich triviale Verfilmung eines Fort/Da-Spieles. Es geht aber hier nicht um die *Bedeutung*, die dieser Film bewusst oder - eher unbewusst transportiert -, sondern es geht um seine konsequente Verlängerung in die *Bedeutungslosigkeit*. Das ist die Arbeit seiner Transformation in eine neue Form. Bedeutungen im Film verschwinden machen, heißt vor allem, sprechende Personen zum Verschwinden oder zum Schweigen zu bringen. Jemanden nicht sehen, wo er nach der ‚Logik' des Films

be it only as a potemkinian façade, is, in the other shape, virtually capable of being created from within the apparatus itself. Inasmuch as the digital medium allows for the artificial induction of every dot of the image, calling-up, in the process, almost any object at will, one is no longer faced with the clumsiness of the analogue medium where everything, somehow, had to be actually built and dragged up before the camera.

But the process, by which something can be presented, can also be inverted. Naturally it didn't take long for the discovery to be arrived at that a film needed merely to be arrested for something to be excised from it, which, upon restarting, would appear as *vanished*. In contrast to occurrences in the real world, a strip of film may be *cut*. But, so far, we are still dealing with the physical space of a corporeal medium, which can only grasp the actual process from the outside. The change to the medium of interior processing, of the sort made possible by the electronic creation of images, by its very nature changes the relationship to the image as such, or more precisely, to the content of the image. The electronic tool interferes with the narrative itself.

The film re-worked and altered by Martin Arnold, *The Invisible Ghost*, depicts, true to its title, multiple forms of disappearance and re-apperance. There is, for one, the vanished wife whose portrait hangs in the vestibule of the house and which is later mutilated. Again and again she re-emerges from her seclusion, only to trigger off another form of disappearance, the trance, the dimming of her husband's clear consciousness, who, as soon as he catches a glimpse of her at the window, is swallowed up by the vortex of his madness and goes about causing the disappearance of young girls or even the gardener, i. e., extinguishing them, killing them. After the deed is done, he returns to his own mind, to consciousness, regretfully taking note that his action, which he does not *recognise* as having been perpetrated by him, is now causing his daughter's boy-friend to vanish. The young lad is found guilty of the deed and promptly executed, only to reappear, soon after, in the shape of his own brother to whom he bears a deceptive similarity.

One could discover further series of this kind and conclude that the film offers nothing more than a fairly trivial rendition of a game of *Fort/Da* [Freud's name for the perennial childhood favourite of "Peek-a-Boo".] However, the emphasis here is not on the *significance* which the film consciously - or rather, subconsciously - conveys, what is more to the point is its consistent extension towards *insignificance*. That is the achievement of its transformation into a new form. Causing significances in a film to vanish, means, above all, that one has to cause speaking characters to vanish, by silencing them. Not to be seeing someone in a place where, according to the film's inner "logic", he ought to be

sein müsste, jemanden sehen, der die Lippen geschlossen hält, obwohl er nach der ‚Logik' des Films reden müsste - brutaler lässt sich die ‚Logik' des Films, d. h. seine Aufdringlichkeit des Erzählens, nicht zerstören. Es scheint demnach, wie wenn zunächst nur eine jener Paradoxien aufgehoben würde, die in dieser besagten ‚Logik' des Films liegen, nämlich, dass uns seine Erzählung daran hindert, den Grund dafür zu sehen. Die Erzählung eines Filmes *auslöschen*, indem man ihre Darsteller verschwinden macht, das verweist auf eine Entleerung des Bildes, die gleichwohl nicht die Leere zum Vorschein bringen kann. Schließlich können wir das Gedankenexperiment wagen, alle Gegenstände aus einem Raum uns als verschwunden zu denken. Etwas wird bleiben müssen, solange wir in der Anschaulichkeit bleiben wollen. Wir können nicht ‚nichts' sehen. Im Film nun muss diese Leere genauso wie die Fülle hergestellt werden.

Georges Didi-Huberman hat uns auf den Unterschied aufmerksam gemacht, der zwischen dem Sichtbaren und dem *Visuellen* liegt. Bevor wir durch Albertis Fenster zu blicken gelernt haben, um in die Sichtbarkeit von Geschichten eingeübt zu werden, existierte eine andere Sehweise, die sich in der religiösen Malerei verkörperte. Sie liegt vor unserem medialen Nullpunkt, der durch die Erfindung und Etablierung der Zentralperspektive geschaffen wurde, und verfolgt ein völlig anderes bildliches Konzept. In diesem erlangt das, was uns als das verhältnismäßig Gleichgültige gilt, nämlich der Hintergrund, der allen Figuren scheinbar nur als Träger dient, erhöhte Wichtigkeit. Er kann auch in einem anderen Sinne als *Grund* des auf ihm Erscheinenden gedacht werden, insofern ihm eine Potenz zugesprochen wird. In der aristotelischen Tradition spielt „der Ort keineswegs bloß die Rolle eines mehr oder minder neutralen und unbestimmten ‚Behälters' der Formen."[3] Der Ort ist gegenüber den Figuren und Formen nicht gleichgültig. „Die Figuren, die Formen, bewohnen nicht einfach einen Ort, sie werden von ihm *produziert*."[4] Damit stehen die Figuren, welche die *Erzählung* tragen, in einem vertikalen Verhältnis zum Hintergrund, mit dem sie nicht gleichwertig sind. Es eröffnet sich somit eine gewisse Tiefe, eine Staffelung der Bildfläche, eine Dimensionalität, die nicht einfach körperlich und somit wiederum dem Sichtbaren unterworfen ist. Das Visuelle konstituiert sich im Gegensatz zum Sichtbaren durch seine Potentialität, es weist aus dem Bild heraus und verweist gleichzeitig auf die Bedingung aller Bilder. Bedingung nicht im Sinne ihrer Herstellbarkeit, sondern hinsichtlich ihrer Weise des Bedeutens. In einem anderen Kontext und mit anderer Absicht taucht das Problem Jahrhunderte später wieder auf, als Künstler der amerikanischen Avantgarde der 1950er Jahre Objekte konzipieren, die von der Zerstörung, vom Verschwinden der Objekte sprechen. Hier nun stoßen wir auf das Problem: „Wie zeigt man Leere? Und

standing, or seeing someone whose lips are sealed, even though, again "logically", he should be speaking - it becomes hard to imagine a more brutal disruption of the "conclusiveness" of film, of the obtrusive nature of its narrative. It appears, therefore, as if, initially, merely one of the paradoxes had been cancelled out, which is inherent in this very "logic" of the film, i. e., the fact that its narrative obstructs our perception of the grounds that it is based on. *Extinguishing* the narrative of a film by causing its actors to vanish leads to a draining of the image, which nevertheless cannot cause the emptiness to come to light. After all, we can engage in the mental experiment of imagining all objects in a room to have vanished. Yet something will need to be retained, as long as we wish to remain within the sphere of vividness and clarity. We cannot see 'nothing'. In a film, this emptiness must be created precisely the same as must be the profusion of objects.

Georges Didi-Huberman has alerted us to the distinction that lies between the visible and the *visual*. Before we learnt to gaze out of *Alberti's Window*, to become practised in the visibility of stories, a different way of seeing existed, which was embodied in religious painting. It stretches out before our point X marking the zero of media development, which was created by the invention and establishment of the central perspective, and pursues a completely different pictorial concept. In it, the element which counts as a matter of relative indifference to us, i.e., the background, which merely serves as a carrier-medium for all figures, acquires a heightened importance. It can also be thought of, in a different sense, as the *ground* for all that appears upon it, in as much as a potency is ascribed to it. In the Aristotelian tradition, "location by no means plays a mere role as the more or less neutral or indefinite 'container' of all shapes."[3] Location is not indifferent in relation to figures and shapes. "The figures, the shapes, do not simply inhabit a place, they are *produced* by it."[4] This said, the characters which transport the *narrative* stand in a vertical relationship to the background, without being of equal value to it. What is opened up, then, is a certain depth, a grading of the picture plane, a dimensionality, which is not simply physical and is therefore, in turn, subject to what is visible. The visual constitutes itself, in contrast to the visible, through its potentiality, it points beyond the picture while at the same time referring to the condition of all pictures. Condition not in the sense of their manufacturability, but with regard to their manner of signification. In another context and with a different intention the problem reappears again, centuries later, when artists of the American avant-garde of the 1950s were conceptualising objects, which spoke of the destruction, of the disappearance, of objects. Here now we are confronted with the problem: "How do you show emptiness? And how do you create a shape from such an act of showing - a shape which gazes back at us?"[5] Something

wie macht man aus diesem Akt eine Form - eine Form, die uns anblickt?"[5] Etwas, das uns anblickt, das heißt: über seine bloße Sichtbarkeit hinaus uns betrifft und beunruhigt.

Wir nähern uns dem Nullpunkt jedes Bildmediums. Es kann nicht nichts zeigen, ohne sich selbst auszulöschen. Seine Leere ist der *Hintergrund*, sein Nullzeichen. Im Falle zu langer Belichtungszeiten bei Photo und Film sehen wir das sich zu schnell Bewegende nicht, aber doch den stillstehenden Hintergrund, der gleichsam eine Substanz ist, die in der Zeit beharrt. Dieser zeigt uns neben seiner spezifischen Gestalt doch gleichzeitig, dass in gewisser Weise nichts sich abspielt. Das ist beim Film deutlicher als beim Photo, wo jede Bewegung festgefroren ist. Unterschreitet der Film das Niveau des Bildes, dann wird der Projektor zur bloßen Lichtquelle, er hat sich als Medium verabschiedet. Um als solches sich zu erhalten, bedarf es zumindest der kleinsten transportierten Nachricht. Man wird sich vielleicht an die experimentellen „Fadenfilme" erinnern, wo nicht viel mehr als ein sich windender Faden zu sehen war, der nun nicht zufällig vor die Linse kam, sondern als jener infinitesimale Punkt der Differenz von Licht und Medium gelten konnte. Es gibt also vielleicht einen semantischen Nullpunkt des Films, der schon wesentlich bildgesättigter ist und uns eine Hintergrundszenerie zeigt, wie wir sie für bestimmte Genres erwarten: Die Wüstenstadt für den Western, finstere Häuser für den Grusel- oder Kriminalfilm, technizistische für den Science Fiction Film, und so weiter. Dieser semantische Nullpunkt des Films ist selber nicht Teil einer bestimmten filmischen Erzählung, aber doch die Bedingung jeder solchen Erzählung.

Brian Rotman hat das arithmetische Nullzeichen - welches die Leere anzeigt, als Zeichen bedeutet, dass an dieser Stelle kein anderes Zahlzeichen steht, also nicht nichts ist - mit dem Fluchtpunkt in der Zentralperspektive verglichen. Der Fluchtpunkt bezeichnet die äußerste Tiefe der perspektivischen Konstruktion, misst die Dimension des Hintergrundes aus. Das immer getreue Grimmsche Wörterbuch bestätigt uns unter dem Stichwort „Hintergrund" die Beziehung zur Zentralperspektive, insofern es sich um einen in der Malerei und der Bühnenkunst gebräuchlichen Ausdruck handelt. Man wird sich erinnern, dass die Zentralperspektive auch „Theaterperspektive" genannt wurde, eben wegen ihrer Verwendung in der Kulissenmalerei. Das Wörterbuch bemüht hier einige Male den unvergleichlichen Medientheoretiker Goethe, der den Übergang von der Bühne in die Metaphorik ausdeutet, indem er diese hintergeht: „was [in einem drama] auszer dem theater vorgeht, was der zuschauer nicht sieht, was er sich vorstellen musz, ist wie ein hintergrund, vor dem die spielenden figuren sich bewegen."[6] Sie bewegen sich demnach vor einem doppelten Hintergrund, nämlich einem sichtbaren und einem virtuellen. Sie stellen die Verbindung zwischen diesen beiden

that looks back at us, i.e., which affects us and disturbs us beyond its mere visibility.

We are approaching point zero of any pictorial medium. It cannot show nothing without extinguishing itself. Its emptiness is the *background,* its symbol for zero. In the case of too slow an exposure in film and photography we can no longer make out any object that moves too rapidly, but we can see the background standing still, almost like a substance, wherein time persists. The background, besides its specific shape, shows us, at the same time, that in a certain way there is nothing taking place. This becomes more easily apparent in film than in photography, where every movement is frozen fast. If the film falls short at the level of the picture, the projector becomes a mere source of light, taking leave of its function as a medium. To preserve a semblance of that function, it requires at least the smallest of transmitted messages. One may recollect the experimental "string films" of the past, where not much more was to be seen than a wriggling piece of string, which did not, however, come before the lens accidentally, but could rather be viewed as that very infinitesimal point of difference between light and the medium. So there may indeed exist a semantic zero ground of film, which is substantially more image-saturated and shows us a background scenery of the sort we would expect in certain genres, the desert town of the western, sinister houses for the horror- or crime-film, technological whizz-bang stuff for the science-fiction film, and so forth. This semantic zero-point of film is itself not a part of a specific cinematographic narrative, yet it is the precondition of any such narrative.

Brian Rotman has compared the arithmetic symbol of zero - which indicates emptiness and as a symbol points to the fact that no other numerical symbol occupies its slot, and so therefore does not signify nothing - to the vanishing point in central perspective. The vanishing point refers to the greatest depth in the construction of perspective, measuring the dimension of the background. The ever-faithful Grimm's Dictionary of the German Language, under the entry headed "background", corroborates our view regarding a link to the central perspective, in as far as a term commonly used in painting and stagecraft is concerned. It will be remembered that the central perspective used also to be referred to as the "theatrical perspective", precisely because of its use in backdrop painting. The dictionary here, on several occasions, calls upon the splendid services of that incomparable media theoretician, Goethe, who fully interprets the term's transition from the stage to metaphorics, by circumnavigating it: "...what (in a play) happens outside the theatre, and what the spectator does not see, what is left to his imagination, is like a background against which the playing characters are seen to be moving."[6] The actors, as a consequence, move against a dual backdrop, a visible one, and a

Bedingungsräumen her, die sich selbst nicht vermitteln können, weil sie streng getrennt sind.

Vor einem Hintergrund agieren im Film „handelnde Personen", deren gebräuchlichste Identifizierung, wie auch im Alltagsleben, über ihr Gesicht geleistet wird. Gesichter stellen den semantischen Nullpunkt des nicht-wissenschaftlichen, also unterhaltenden Filmes dar, der ja nicht wenig - zumindest seit Einführung des Tonfilms - auf der Rede basiert. Das Gesicht begleitet die Rede, wie sie physisch aus dem Hintergrund des Gesichtes entspringt. Das Gesicht ist das inter-face zur Welt, über es läuft alle Verbindung zu den anderen [Gesichtern]. Man könnte nun medientechnisch einen Rückschritt zum Stummfilm dergestalt ins Werk setzen, als die begleitende Tonspur nur ein dauerndes Rauschen, aber keine Nachricht übermittelt. Solches aber wird nicht zum bildlichen Ausdruck. Wenn wir aber Gesichter sehen, deren Mund sich nicht öffnet, obwohl alles dies zu verlangen scheint, dann ist die Stimme gleichsam in den Abgrund gedrängt. Wie auf bestimmten mittelalterlichen Bildern der Engel der Verkündigung seine Botschaft mit geschlossenem Mund überbringt, so teilt sich hier das Medium mit. Aber anders als beim Engel handelt es sich nicht um eine Frohbotschaft. Was es zeigt, „ist das menschliche Schweigen, die Unterbrechung des Diskurses, die Angst erzeugt und jene ‚Einsamkeit zu zweit', die Sterbende oder Verrückte durch ihre Gegenwart mit sich bringen"[7]. Die Dominanz unseres Blickes entgleitet uns, das gesehene Objekt schärft seinen auf uns geworfenen Blick, unterwirft uns der Macht des Unheimlichen. In der bildlichen Stille dieses Aktes wird uns bedeutet, dass nicht nur wir in ihm sein Erlöschen sehen, sondern dass es unseren Blick und uns überleben wird. Denn wir sind einfach und die Medien sind vielfach.

virtual one. They represent the juncture between these two conditional spaces which cannot, themselves, communicate with one another, as they are domiciled in rigidly separate camps.

In films the "leading players" are seen acting against a background and their most customary method of identification, as in everyday life, is achieved via their faces. Faces represent the semantic exact zero of the non-scientific, i.e., entertaining film, which is based not a little - at least since the introduction of the soundtrack in films - on human speech. The face accompanies such speech just as it does physically emerge from the background of the face. The face is the point of intersection with the world, a terminal that can be read, and which connects with all the other faces. Inverting the progress in media technology, one might go back to the silent era, of sorts, by filling the soundtrack with a continuous white noise, transporting no message. But such an action would leave the pictorial expression unaffected. If, however, we see faces, whose mouths do not open, even though everything appears to call for it, then the voice has been, in a manner of speaking, pushed into the abyss. Just as in certain medieval pictures the Angel of Annunciation delivers his message with his mouth closed, so, too, does the medium communicate itself here. But unlike the angel, it does not deliver a message of joy. What it shows "is a human silence, the interruption of discourse, which generates fear, and that certain 'solitude of two', which the dying or the crazy instil in us by their mere presence."[7] The dominance of our gaze slips away from us, the seen object sharpens its reflected glance upon us, subjecting us to the power of the uncanny. In the pictorial silence of this act we are given to understand that it is not only us who can see its exctinction within it, but that it will survive our gaze as well as us. For we are just a one and the media are the many.

| 1 Thomas Bernhard: Auslöschung. Ein Zerfall, Frankfurt: Suhrkamp 1988, S. 199 | 2 a.a.O., S. 128. | 3 Georges Didi-Huberman: Fra Angelico. Unähnlichkeit und Figuration. Aus dem Französischen übersetzt von Andreas Knop, München: Fink 1995, S. 23. | 4 Ebd. | 5 Georges Didi-Huberman: Was wir sehen blickt uns an. Zur Metapsychologie des Bildes. Aus dem Französischen von Markus Sedlaczek, München: Fink 1999, S. 18. | 6 Deutsches Wörterbuch, Art.: "Hintergrund", Band 10, Leipzig 1877 (Nachdruck München: dtv 1984), Sp. 1503 | 7 Georges Didi-Huberman: Was wir sehen blickt uns an. Zur Metapsychologie des Bildes. Aus dem Französischen von Markus Sedlaczek, München: Fink 1999, S. 108.

| 1 Thomas Bernhard: [Extinction. A Disintegration], Frankfurt: Suhrkamp 1988, p. 199 | 2 ibid., p. 128 | 3 Georges Didi-Huberman: [Fra Angelico. Dissimilarity and Figuration. Translated from the French by Andreas Knop] Munich: Fink 1995, p. 23 {Fra Angelico - Dissemblance et Figuration, 1990} | 4 ibid. | 5 Georges Didi-Huberman: [What We See Looks Back at Us. On the Meta-Psychology of the Image. From the French by Markus Sedlaczek] Munich: Fink 1999, p. 18 {Ce que nous voyons, ce qui nous regarde, 1992} | 6 [German Dictionary, Article on 'Background', Vol. 10, Leipzig 1877 (Reprint Munich: dtv 1984)] Section 1503 | 7 Georges Didi-Huberman: [What We See Looks Back at Us. On the Meta-Psychology of the Image. From the French by Markus Sedlaczek] Munich: Fink 1999, p. 108

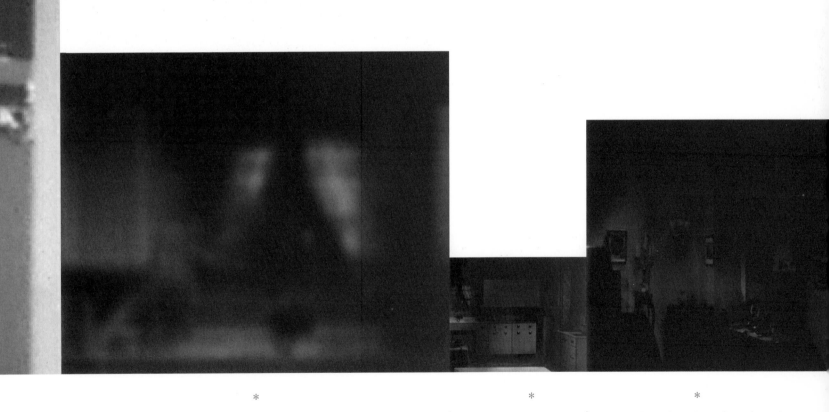

*　　　*　　*
· · · I · I · · I · · · I · · · · · · · · · · · · · · · · ·

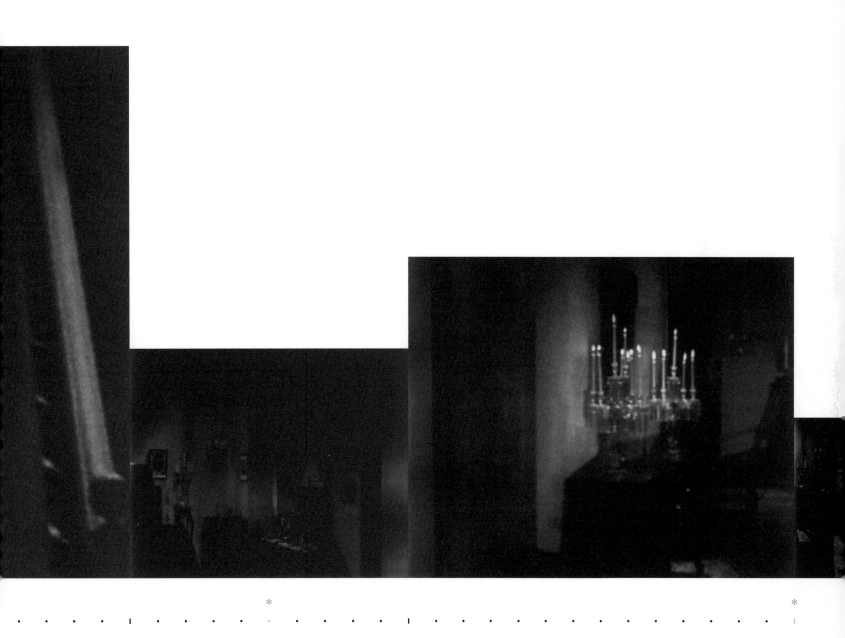

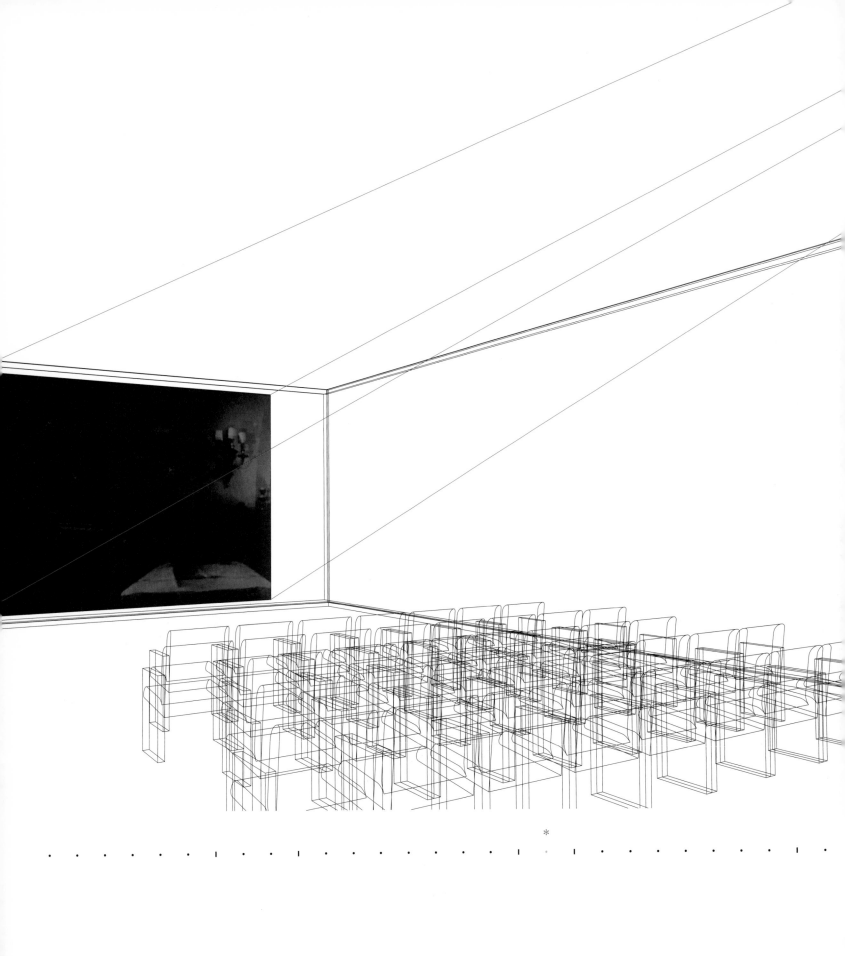

*
· · · · · · · · · · | · | · | · · · · · · · · | · · · | · | · · · · · · · · | ·

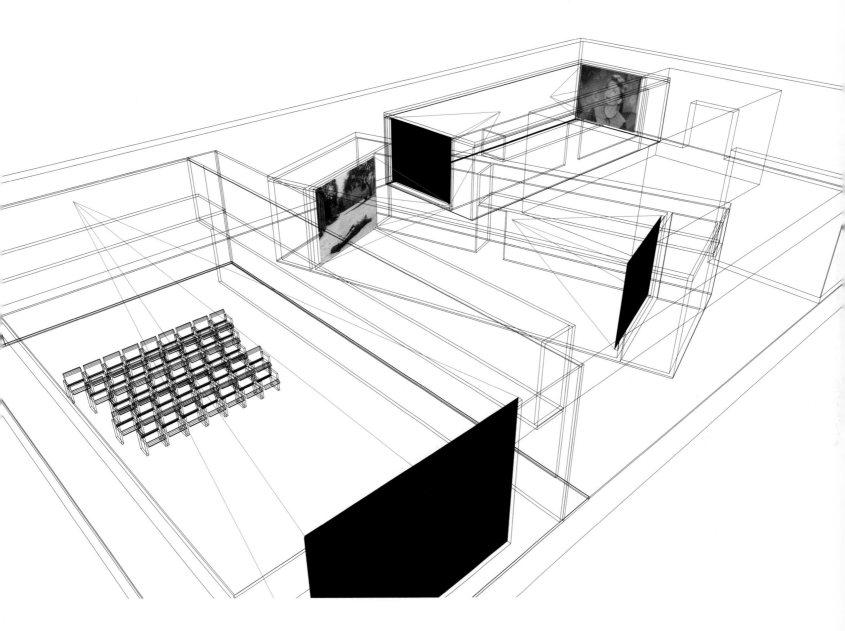

FORSAKEN, 2002

Schwarzweiß-Film auf DVD, 4-Kanal Ton
Rauminstallation, 2 Projektionsflächen 4 x 3 m
Loop-Dauer: 9 min |

Black-and-white film on DVD, 4-channel sound
Spatial installation, 2 projection screens 4 x 3 m
Loop duration: 9 min

DISSOCIATED, 2002

Schwarzweiß-Film auf DVD, 4-Kanal Ton
Rauminstallation, 2 Projektionsflächen 4 x 3 m
Loop-Dauer: 8 min |

Black-and-white film on DVD, 4-channel sound
Spatial installation, 2 projection screens 4 x 3 m
Loop duration: 8 min

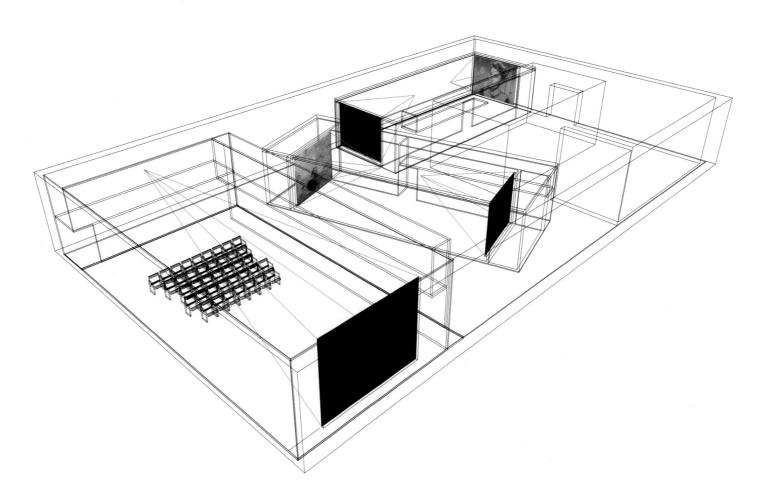

*

Martin Arnold

1959	Geboren in Wien	Born in Vienna
1979-87	Studium der Psychologie und Kunst-geschichte an der Universität Wien	Studied Psychology and Art History at Vienna University
seit 1987 since	Freischaffender Filmemacher	self-employed filmmaker
1996	Gastprofessur an der University of Wisconsin, Milwaukee	Guest Professor at the University of Wisconsin, Milwaukee
1997	1998	Gastprofessur am San Francisco Art Institute	Guest Professor at the San Francisco Art Institute
1999	Gastprofessur an der Städelschule, Frankfurt	Guest Professor at the Städelschule, Frankfurt
2000	2001	Gastprofessur am Bard College, New York	Guest Professor at Bard College, New York

* Certificate of Merit Winner. New Visions. San Francisco Int. Film Festival 1999

* Best Animated Film Award. Ann Arbor Film Festival 1999

* Best of the New Screen. Images Festival. Windsor. Canada. 1999

* Großer Preis. Int. Kurzfilmtage Oberhausen 1998

* Preis der Jury der Int. Filmkritik. Int. Kurzfilmtage Oberhausen 1998

* 2. Preis. Low Budget Film Festival. Hamburg 1998

* 1. Preis. Teplice Film Festival 1998

* Preis für Innovatives Kino. Diagonale 1998

* UK Arena Audience Award. Pandaemonium Festival. London 1998

* Second Prize. Cinema Texas. Austin 1998

* Second Prize. New York Film & Video Expo 1998

* Würdigungspreis für Filmkunst. Land Niederösterreich 1995

* Most Technically Innovative Film. Ann Arbor 1994

* Judge's Choice Award. Humboldt Film Festival 1994

* Jury Member Award. Humboldt Film Festival 1994

* Primo Premio. Arco Madrid 1994

* Grande Premio de Curta Metragem. Figueira da Foz 1994

* Würdigungspreis für Filmkunst. Republik Österreich 1994

* 1. Preis der Jury. Low Budget Film Festival Hamburg 1993

* Certificate of Merit. Cork Film Festival 1993

* Preis für Junges Kino. Viennale 1993

* Primo Premio. Arco Madrid 1992

* Golden Gate Award. New Visions. San Francisco Int. Film Festival 1990

* Gold Award (exp. cat.). Houston Int. Film Festival 1990

* Best of the Festival. Ann Arbor Film Festival 1990

* Best of the Category (exp.) Athens Film Festival 1990

* Certificate of Merit Award. Chicago Int. Film Festival 1990

* Förderungspreis des Adolf Schärf Fonds 1990

2001
Brooklyn Academy of Music |
San Francisco Cinematheque |
Museum of Fine Arts. Boston |
Museo de Bellas Artes.Buenos Aires |
International Film Festival. Jerusalem |
Cinémathèque Française. Paris |
Lux Center. London |
Museum für Gestaltung. Zürich |
Kunsthalle Bielefeld |

2000
San Francisco Art Institute |
Chicago Art Institute |
Pleasure Dome. Toronto |
Auditorium du Louvre. Paris |
Musée National d'Art Moderne. Centre Georges Pompidou. Paris |
Tate Modern. London |
Institut for Contemporary Art. London |
Kunstmuseum. Bern |
Österreichisches Filmmuseum. Wien |

1999
PS1. Brooklyn |
San Francisco International Film Festival |
Filmforum. Los Angeles |
Museum of Fine Arts. Houston |
Museum of Fine Arts. Portland |
International Film Festival. Toronto |
Image Forum Festival. Tokyo |
International Film Festival. Cannes |
Centre d'Art Contemporain. Grenoble |

1998
New York Film Festival |
New York Expo of Film & Video |
Harvard Film Archive. Cambridge |
Musée National d'Art Moderne. Centre Georges Pompidou. Paris |
Cinémathèque Française. Paris |
London International Film Festival |
Rotterdam International Film Festival |
Nederlands Filmmuseum. Amsterdam |

1997
Anthology Film Archives. New York |
Cleveland Cinematheque |
Museum of Modern Art. Denver |
Museum of Fine Arts. Boston |
Image Forum. Tokyo |
Cinémathèque Royale. Bruxelles |
Internationales Filmfestival. Locarno |
Kino Arsenal. Berlin | Kinemathek. Bonn |

1996
San Francisco Cinematheque |
Pacific Film Archives. Berkeley |
Saitama Arts Theatre. Tokyo |
Kinomuseum. Moskau |
Musée National d'Art Moderne. Centre Georges Pompidou. Paris |
Soros Centre for the Arts. Ljubliana |
Danske Filminstitut. Kopenhagen |
Sprengel Museum. Hannover |
Österreichisches Filmmuseum. Wien |

Ausgewählte Bibliografie | Selected Bibliography

1995
Museum of Modern Art. New York |
Anthology Film Archives. New York |
Pacific Film Archives. Berkeley |
Kemper Museum. Kansas City |
Hirschhorn Museum. Washington |
Jeu de Paume. Paris |
Musée des Beaux-Arts. Lyon |
Institute for Contemporary Arts. London |
Kunsthalle St. Gallen |

1994
Anthology Film Archives. New York |
Millenium. New York |
Museum of the Moving Image. Queens |
National Gallery of Art. Washington |
Sao Paolo Film Festival |
Cinémathèque Francaise. Paris |
Nederlands Filmmuseum. Amsterdam |
Kino Arsenal. Berlin |
Museum Weserburg. Bremen |

1993
New York Film Festival |
San Francisco Cinematheque |
Nelson Atkins Museum. Kansas City |
Melbourne International Film Festival |
National Film Festival. London |
Filmoteca Espagnola. Madrid |
Museo De Bellas Artes. Bilbao |
Museo National Centro de Arte. Valencia |
Kunsthalle. Basel |
Galerie Porticus. Frankfurt |

1992
Art Institute. Chicago |
Media Arts Center. Salt Lake City |
Musée National d'Art Moderne.
Centre Georges Pompidou. Paris |
Espace d'Art Contemporain. Lyon |
Fondation d'Art Contemporain. Montpellier |
Arco. Madrid |
Filminstitut. Düsseldorf |
Filmhaus. Aachen |

1991
Brooklyn Museum |
Cleveland Cinémathèque |
Hirshhorn Museum. Washington |
Museum of Fine Arts. Richmond |
International Film Festival. Melbourne |
International Film Festival. Sidney |
National Film Theatre. London |
Museum für Moderne Kunst. Zagreb |
Olympisches Museum. Sarajewo |

1990
New York Film Festival |
San Francisco International Film Festival |
Pacific Film Archives. Berkeley |
Chicago International Film Festival |
Houston International Film Festival |
Denver International Film Festival |
International Film Festival. Cannes |
Media Art Festival. Osnabrück |
Müszarnok. Budapest |

* **Delorme, Stéphane:** Found footage, mode démploi.
In: Cahiers du Cinema. Numéro Hors-Série, Paris, May 2000.

* **Rosenbaum, Jonathan:** Wrinkles in Time.
In: Chicago Weekly Reader. Chicago, February 18, 2000.

* **Waniek, Eva:** Le cinema et les corps: un art du luxe.
In: Beauvais, Yann & Collin, Jean-Damien (eds.):
Florilège Scratch. Scratch, Paris, October 1999.

* **Morris, Gary:** Compulsion at 24 frames per second.
Film of Martin Arnold at Cinematheque. In: The Bay Area
Reporter. Vol. 29 No 12, San Francisco, March 1999.

* **Huston, Johnny Ray:** What makes you tic / Out loud.
In: San Francisco Bay Guardian. Vol. 33 No. 25,
San Francisco, March 1999

* **Noetinger, Jérome:** Martin Arnold. In: revue & corrigée.
Trimestrial, numéro 39, Grenoble, April 1999, pp. 29 - 31.

* **Kermabon, Jacques:** Martin Arnold, Scratcher Hollywood.
In: Bref. Le magazine du court métrage. Nr. 40,
Paris printemps 1999, pp. 16 - 21.

* **Sallmann, Berhard:** Anmerkungen zum neuen
österreichischen Filmschaffen.
Filmforum - Zeitschrift für Film und andere Künste. Berlin,
Heft 14, November/Dezember 1998.

* **MacDonald, Scott:** Martin Arnold.
In: A Critical Cinema: Interviews with Independant Film-
makers. University of California Press, Berkeley /
Los Angeles / London 1998, pp. 347 - 362.

* **Korschil, Thomas:** Konterbande Über einige neue kürzere
und längere Filme in Österreich.
In: Meteor. Teste zum Laufbild. Sondernummer Diagonale
1998 PVS Verleger, Wien 1998.

* **Philipp, Claus:** Die modellierte Einsamkeit.
In: Der Standard, Wien, 20. März 1998.

* **Grissemann, Stefan:** Maschinelle Erregungen.
In: Die Presse, Wien, 19. März 1998.

* **Omasta, Michael:** Die Ordnung der Dinge.
In: Der Falter, Nr. 12, Wien 1998, S. 18 - 19.

* **Lippit, Akira M.:** Martin Arnold's Memory Machine.
In: Afterimage. The Journal of Media Arts and Cultural
Criticism. Vol. 24 No. 6, Rochester, NY 1997, pp. 8 -10.

* **Korschil, Thomas:** Iz Arhiva / Out of the Archive.
The Reinvention of the Past. In: Borcic, Barabara, et al.:
medij v mediju / media in media (Katalog slow./dt.).
Ljublijana 1997, pp. 134 - 145.

* **MacDonald, Scott:** Martin Arnold. In: Centre Georges
Pompidou (ed.): L'art du mouvement. Collection cinéma-
thographique du Musée nationale d'art moderne.
1919 - 1996. Catalogue sous la direction de Jean-Michael
Bohours. Paris 1996, pp. 32 - 33.

* **Grissemann, Stefan:** Martin Arnold. Don't. Der Öster-
reichfilm. Mysterienmaschine. In: Polyfilm Verleih (Hg.):
Eine Geschichte der Bilder. Acht Found Footage Filme
aus Österreich. Katalog. Wien 1996, S. 22 - 30.

* **Tscherkassky, Peter:** Brève histoire du cinema
d'avantgarde autrichien.
In: Centre Pompidou (ed.): L'avant-garde autrichienne
au cinéma 1955 - 1993. Paris 1996, pp.15 - 32.

* **Turim, Maureen C.:** Eine Begegnung mit dem Bild.
Martin Arnolds "pièce touchée". In: Horwath, Alexander
/ Ponger, Lisl / Schlemmer, Gottfried (Hg.): Avantgardefilm
Österreich. 1950 bis heute. Verlag Wespennest,
Wien 1995, S. 301 - 307.

* **MacDonald, Scott:** Sp.. Sp.. Spaces of Inscription.
Scott MacDonald im Gespräch mit Martin Arnold. (dt. Über-
setzung). In: Horwath, Alexander / Ponger, Lisl / Schlemmer,
Gottfried (Hg.): Avantgardefilm Österreich. 1950 bis heute.
Verlag Wespennest, Wien 1995, S. 284 - 300.

* **Tscherkassky, Peter:** Die rekonstruierte Kinematografie.
Zur Filmavantgarde in Österreich. In: Horwath, Alexander
/ Ponger, Lisl / Schlemmer, Gottfried (Hg.):
Avantgardefilm Österreich. 1950 bis heute. Verlag
Wespennest, Wien 1995, S. 9 - 92.

* **Philipp, Claus:** Tanz mit Fundstücken. Martin Arnold und
seine Filme. In: Illetschko, Peter (Hg.): Gegenschuß.
Verlag Wespennest, Wien 1995, S. 24 - 38.

* **Grissmann, Stefan:** Das Arnold Syndrom. In:
Kulturpreisträger des Landes Niederösterreich.
Katalog. 1995, S. 20-21

* **Tscherkassky, Peter:** hand made. Avantgardefilm in
Österreich. In: Media Biz. Wien März 1995, S. 16 - 17.

* **MacDonald, Scott:** Sp.. Sp.. Spaces of Inscription:
An interview with Martin Arnold.
In: Film Quaterly. Vol 48 No. 1, Fall 1994, pp. 3 - 11.

* **Stadler, Hilar:** Das Physische des Kinos:
Über 2 Filme von Martin Arnold.
In: Das Kunst Bulletin. Nr.3, Kriens 1994, S. 54 - 56.

* **Tscherkassky, Peter:** The Light of Peripherie. A brief history
of Austrian Avant-Garde Cinema. In: Austrian Avant-Garde
Cinema 1955 - 1993 (catalogue). Wien 1994, pp. 11 - 24.

* **Jutz, Gabriele:** Pièce touchée ou l'espace filmique reécrit.
In: dies.: Espace et Cinéma d' Avant-Garde Autrichien.
In: Sémiotiques. Nr. 4, Paris Juni 1993, S. 81 - 84.

* **Grissemann, Stefan:** Metal Beat. Methoden der
Verstümmelung und Neuordnung in Martin Arnolds Film
„passage à l'acte". In: Blimp. Zeitschrift für Film Nr.22 / 23,
Graz 1993, S. 10 - 12.

* **Reumüller, Barbara & Roth, Michael:** Wider-holungen.
Ein Gespräch mit Martin Arnold. In: Filmfolder Nr. 55,
Wien 2/1993, S. 4 - 7.

Ausstellungsliste |
List of exhibited works

* **Philipp, Claus:** Neuland zwischen den Bildkadern.
Zur Weltpremiere von Martin Arnolds Found Footage Film
„Passage à l'acte". In: Der Standard, Wien 3. März 1993.

* **Weixelbaumer, Robert:** Familie Hollywood auf der Couch.
Avantgarde-Filmemacher Martin Arnold über seine neue
Arbeit „passage à l'acte". In: Die Presse, Wien 4. März 1993.

* **Praschl, Bernhard:** Hollywood, mit dem Seziermesser
traktiert. Martin Arnolds Filme laufen Amok.
In: Kurier, 4. März 1993.

* **Robnik, Drehli:** Vom Tick zum Stottern.
In: Der Falter, Nr. 9, Wien 1993.

* **Staretz, David:** Martin Arnold. Hermetisches Knattern.
In: Lauda Air Magazin. Ausg. 2, Wien 1993.

* **Tscherkassky, Peter:** Die Analogien der Avantgarde.
In: Hausheer, Cecilia & Settele, Christoph (Hg.):
Found Footage Film. Viper / Zyklop Verlag.
Luzern 1992, S. 26 - 35.

* **Tscherkassky, Peter:** Filmavantgarde in Österreich.
In: Bono, Francesco (Hg.): Austria (In)felix. Zum öster-
reichischen Film der 80ger Jahre.
Edition Blimp: Graz / Aiace. Rom 1992, S. 42 - 60.

* **Martin Arnold** im Gespräch mit **Blimp** über seinen Film
„pièce touchée". In: Wieser-Huber, Judith & Wieser,
Ralph (Hg.): Filmbrunch 1 - 19. Katalog.
Wien 1992, S. 40 - 41.

* **Tscherkassky, Peter:** Wirkliche Filme oder: Gibt es ein
nicht-fiktionales Kino? In: Blimp. Zeitschrift für Film.
Nr. 16, Frühjahr 1991, S. 38 - 42.

* **Illetschko, Peter:** Tanz der Bilder. Über den österreichischen
Experimentalfilm „pièce touchée". In: Parnaß Art Magazine.
Nr. 1, Wien Jan. / Feb. 1990, S. 20.

* **Illmaier, Gerhild & Grbic, Bogdan:** Pièce Touchée on the
Road. Blimp im Gespräch mit dem Avantgardisten der 3.
Generation. In: Blimp. Zeitschrift für Film. Nr. 14,
Sommer 1990, S. 19 - 21.

* **Praschl, Bernhard:** Griff in den Müll. Martin Arnold ist
Österreichs erfolgreichster Experimentalfilmer.
In: Die Presse, Wien 9. / 10. Juni 1990.

* **Stadler, Tina; Zach, Peter & Grbic, Bogdan:** Oeil Touchée.
Blimp im Gespräch mit Peter Tscherkassky & Martin Arnold.
In: Blimp. Zeitschrift für Film. Nr. 13. Graz 1989, S. 26 - 30.

* **Horwath, Alexander:** „Berührt - Geführt":
Heiße Liebe zwischen Technik und Intellekt.
Martin Arnold stellt sein neues Werk vor.
In: Der Standard, 11. Okt. 1989.

Deanimated (The Invisible Ghost), 2002

Schwarzweiß-Film auf DVD, 5-Kanal Ton
Rauminstallation, Projektionsfläche 6 x 4,50 m
Loop-Dauer: 60 min |
Black-and-white film on DVD, 5-channel sound
Spatial installation, projection screen 6 x 4.50 m
Loop duration: 60 min

Forsaken, 2002

Schwarzweiß-Film auf DVD, 4-Kanal Ton
Rauminstallation, 2 Projektionsflächen 4 x 3 m
Loop-Dauer: 9 min |
Black-and-white film on DVD, 4-channel sound
Spatial installation, 2 projection screens 4 x 3 m
Loop duration: 9 min

Dissociated, 2002

Schwarzweiß-Film auf DVD, 4-Kanal Ton
Rauminstallation, 2 Projektionsflächen 4 x 3 m
Loop-Dauer: 8 min |
Black-and-white film on DVD, 4-channel sound
Spatial installation, 2 projection screens 4 x 3 m
Loop duration: 8 min

DEANIMATED - The Invisible Ghost |

FORSAKEN |

DISSOCIATED |

Film / Sound Installationen | **Film / Sound Installations:**
Martin Arnold

Digital Compositing:
Martin Arnold, Matthias Meyer, Roland Seidel,
Harald Hund, Ruth Kaaserer, Fritz Mayer,
Christian Stoppacher, Sophie Thorsen, Philipp Zaufel

Digital Compositing, Assistenz:
Manuel Böck, Christoph Kempter, Almut Rink,
Regine Müller

3D-Matte Animation; Compositing, Supervision:
George Basil

Digital Fusion, Consulting:
mkFX

Digital Fusion, Sponsoring:
Eyeon Software

Projektionstechnische Beratung |
Technique of projection/consultancy:
Martin Walitza

Produktion | **Production:**
AMOUR FOU Filmproduktion
Alexander Dumreicher-Ivanceanu,
Gabriele Kranzelbinder

www.amourfou.at/deanimated

Die Herstellung von "Deanimated" wurde durch Förderungen
des Filmfonds Wien, der Kunstsektion des Bundeskanzleramts
und der Abteilung Kultur und Wissenschaft des Landes
Niederösterreich ermöglicht.